CAPTURING THE MIND OF GOD

A Life-Changing Vision
of Your Future

I Cor. 2:9-10

Rick Thomas

RICK THOMAS

DEDICATION

I would like to dedicate this book to my mom
and dad, Pastors W. W. and Edith Thomas, for
teaching me that *"Eye hath not seen, nor ear heard,
neither have entered into the heart of man, the things
which God hath prepared for them that love him"*
(1 Corinthians 2:9), enabling me to discover
how to *Capture the Mind of God.*

CAPTURING THE MIND OF GOD
Copyright © 2003 by Rick Thomas

ISBN: 0-9740880-0-5
Published by

LIFEBRIDGE
BOOKS
P.O. BOX 49428
CHARLOTTE, NC 28277
Printed in the United States of America.
Cover photo courtesy of the National Aeronautics
and Space Administration. Used by permission.
COVER DESIGN BY JR GRAPHICS

CONTENTS

A Transforming Journey

I f there is one area in most believers' lives that is either neglected, ignored, or unknown, it is the area of *vision*.

When I look back over the years of my ministry, I can state without reservation that I deal with this issue more than any other. After people are saved and desire to serve the Lord by fulfilling His will for their lives, the burning issue and question I'm asked most as a pastor is, "How can I find and know the will of God for my life?"

The answer lies within the word "Vision."

The dictionary defines it as "something that is or has been seen." The spiritual definition is "seeing what God sees." Or as my father, Bishop Woody Thomas, so wisely puts it, *"the me I see is the me I'll be."*

The purpose of this book is to enable you to *"see as God sees."* I want you to capture the heart and mind of God, so that you will be able to live your life based on His destiny and purpose for you.

Know this without question: *You are destined with a purpose. God has a plan for your life that guarantees you absolute and total success.*

As a believer, you should base your spiritual life on God's destiny and purpose, rather than on your natural talents and ideas. Oh, He will certainly use those gifts, but the problem I often find in passionate, self-motivated people is that they have a tendency to establish their own vision and goals based on secular philosophies and worldviews. For this reason they never attain the *vision* God has for them.

Consequently, many people take to the grave songs that have never been sung, books that have never been written, and sermons that have never been preached. Many multi-talented, success-oriented individuals allow a "good idea" to steal the *"God* idea*"* from them. God's Word is absolute truth. He says, *"But as it is written, Eye hath not seen, nor ear heard, neither have entered into the heart of man, the things which God hath prepared* [already has] *for them that love him"* (1Corinthians 2:9).

The Almighty has a purpose and a plan for the life of every Christian. Without a proper understanding of vision, you may never enjoy the full benefits of God's plan for you.

IS THERE MORE TO LIFE?

I recently saw this bumper sticker: *The one with the most toys wins.*

Success by the world's standards is measured by the accumulation of wealth and material possessions – a sizable bank account, a beautiful home and a luxury car. Perhaps you may be one of those who continues to accumulate worldly wealth in order to fulfill a need that never seems to be satisfied. *Things* have not brought your desired happiness.

Do you feel as though you are always striving but never quite attaining that elusive fulfillment? You know there must be more to life; somehow there *has* to be.

- What is this evasive *more* that you seek?
- Has God given you a glimpse of a task or an achievement that He wishes you to do for Him?

■ Have you been trying to achieve success in your
own strength?

Because God has created us, and because we are made in
His image (Genesis 1: 27), our inner spirit yearns for the
Master's plan, His purpose, and His destiny for our lives.
You often hear people say, "I just want to make a difference."
Or, "If I could only know what I am on this earth to accom-
plish."

Perhaps I have just described your condition. Is your life
so confused, hectic, stressful, and demanding that you feel as
though you can't bear having to deal with one more experience that you don't understand? Could this be a result of your
success? Or, is it a result of your failures? Either of these
scenarios can produce the same feeling of being
overwhelmed.

YOUR SPECIAL GIFT

What does God call success? In His eyes, success is His
desire for us to see and fulfill all the abilities and talents He
has placed within us. Paul told the Corinthians, *"But each
man has his own gift from God; one has this gift, another has
that"* (1 Corinthians 7:7 NIV). This doesn't always happen
instantly; it is usually a progressive process.

He wants us to accomplish these gifts to our utmost
potential, both in the natural and the spiritual. Only then will
our hearts and souls be at rest – no more haunting questions,
no more indecision about our purpose here on earth.

Is it possible you don't really believe God wants you to be
successful, either spiritually or in the natural world? Many
people have mistakenly interpreted the teaching of Jesus when
He said, *"It is easier for a camel to go through the eye of a*

needle, than for a rich man to enter into the kingdom of God" (Mark 10:25).

Jesus did not mean that a rich man, who would sell all he has and give to the poor, would consequently go to heaven. Salvation is never earned by divesting oneself of all possessions. The deeper problem is the love of money – being more devoted to possessions than to God. The Lord did not say that it was wrong to be wealthy. The problem is putting wealth above all else.

By incorrectly interpreting Jesus' teachings concerning money, many have developed a spirit of poverty. It becomes a stronghold, or a belief system, which keeps them from knowing God's planned will for their life.

Many people tell me they just can't get past the feeling that it is a sin to be prosperous.

> *Let me assure you that God wants to bless and prosper you in order that you will be a blessing to others.*

The Father's desire for your life includes enabling you to earn money for your personal needs and also to support His plans for worldwide evangelism.

God owns everything. He will increase your resources to be made available for His purposes.

What you are about to read is not simply another self-help motivational book. It's not based on the premise of the kindergarten story of the little engine that said, "I think I can. I think I can!"

My objective is to challenge you to believe the Master has a plan – *just for you!* God says, *"Before I formed thee in the belly I knew thee; and before thou camest forth out of the womb I sanctified thee…"* (Jeremiah 1: 5).

This book will teach you God's principles that are needed to achieve both your natural and spiritual goals. I will share stories of everyday men and women, as well as Biblical people who became successful by never losing sight of their vision.

IT'S NOT TOO LATE!

I pray you will embrace what I am about to say and let it become firmly planted within your spirit. *God does not make mistakes!* He does not create people and then try to figure out what to do with them.

You may feel it is too late in your life for anything important or meaningful to be accomplished. Perhaps you have concluded there has been too much water under the bridge for anything successful to happen. Many look back and see a past filled with sorrow and regret. Some have even been told, "Certain folks just aren't meant to accomplish anything in this life. You will just have to wait until you get to heaven."

Let me assure you – *they are wrong!* I don't care how cluttered the past or how confusing the present; God has a purpose and destiny for you. At any stage of life, a person can know God's will and determine His *vision* for his or her life.

You still have an opportunity to be successful and accomplish incredible deeds for God's Kingdom here on earth. The psalmist David declared, *"I had fainted, unless I had believed to see the goodness of the Lord in the land of the living"* (Psalm 27:13).

There is good news. You *can* discern the vision for your life – no matter your age, educational background, financial status, or track record. It is *never* too late!

SOLVING THE PUZZLE

Achieving your future is somewhat like putting a puzzle together. Remember when you first opened up that box of a 500-piece puzzle? The task seemed overwhelming, didn't it? But you slowly began to pick up each piece, looking at it carefully, placing similar colors together while you searched for corners and straight edges in order to fill in the outline. The process required patience and perseverance.

There are many pieces in the puzzle of life that must be recognized and put together in order to obtain your vision. Many fail in the quest because they don't know how to properly assemble the jigsaw. A puzzle is not completed in a short amount of time, rather each piece is picked up, pondered over and finally tried in quite a few places before just the right fit is found. Neither can you expect to always attain your vision instantly.

I want to teach you how to make the right choices and connect the pieces of the puzzle together until eventually you will behold a beautiful, completed picture. You will see your vision manifested.

STEPPING STONES

It's been said, "No one plans to fail, but many fail to plan." Just because God has promised you something does not mean it is automatically going to come to pass. You must ask yourself, "How imperative is it that I achieve my vision?"

Long-term vision (the completed puzzle) can never be achieved without short-term sight, or what I like to call "stepping stones." Remember, the 500-pieces that had to be put in one by one? With only one piece of the puzzle at a time you can finish the course and attain God's purpose for your life.

There is challenge involved in the fulfillment of your vision. If you're not willing to accept it, you will never receive what the Lord has promised to you.

God will not fail you if you will purpose in your heart to seek first His kingdom for your life. Jesus calls us to *"...seek ye first the kingdom of God, and his righteousness; and all these things shall be added unto you"* (Matthew 6:33).

The best is yet to come!

With that in mind, let's begin a spiritual journey into what I believe will transform your life.

Vision makes the difference – *it determines your destiny.* Remember:

The me I see is the me I'll Be.

CHAPTER 1

VISION DETERMINES DESTINY

Moses had his burning bush. I had my bolt of lighting!
Standing in the bathroom brushing my teeth after a night of drinking and partying, I heard the audible voice of God. *"I've called you in the past, and you have not answered. This is the last time I am going to call you."*

I am sure the ground beneath me was shaking, or maybe I just thought it was. Anyway, God had my undivided attention. Right then and there I gave my heart to Jesus. Even though I had attended church all my life, this was different.

In that moment, God revealed to me His vision for my future – no if's, and's, or but's about it; I belonged to Him, and He had chosen me to be His minister.

PICTURES IN MY MIND

God began to reveal His plan for my life by painting pictures in my mind. He showed me three specific things, which have been the heart of my vision since that time. The Lord said I was to:

1. *Return to Bible college.*
2. *Raise up a church to reach the four corners of the world.*
3. *Build a school that would mentor sons and daughters in the faith.*

What an assignment! How on earth was I going to accomplish this?

I was about to be drafted into the armed services, and the Bible school that I had been attending told me never to return. Talk about batting a thousand!

PARTY! PARTY! PARTY!

I was raised in a Godly Christian home. My father, Bishop Woody Thomas, has been a minister for over 65 years and our family life revolved around the church. I attended services every Sunday and went through all the religious motions, but I was not saved. I had not made the commitment to give my heart to Jesus Christ. I definitely had not given God, total control over my life, nor had I seen any reason why I should.

I graduated from high school and even went to Bible college to please my parents, but I flunked out my freshman year, which did *not* please them. I was nineteen years old and my philosophy of life was party, party, and party some more. After all, I thought I was mature enough to make my own decisions.

The real truth was I had no direction and was getting nowhere fast, except to be drafted for a tour in the army with

Uncle Sam. My vision helped me to understand that God had already opened the door to my future. I realized that ministry is where I could best serve God and my country.

Somehow I had never had an eye-opening revelation about the passage in the Bible where God states He has a plan, purpose and destiny for our lives. *"'For I know the plans I have for you,' declares the Lord, 'plans to prosper you and not to harm you, plans to give you hope and a future.'"* (Jeremiah 29:11 NIV).

I remember reading the scripture during those early days, but just didn't understand how it applied to me. Needless to say, I have read it many, many times since to make sure it was firmly planted in my spirit.

There I was with this incredible vision and seemingly no earthly way to fulfill it. Every circumstance indicated that what the Lord allowed me to see was going to be an impossible task to fulfill in the natural realm. First, the school would have to readmit me, and my folks would have to approve. Second, an impending military draft was staring me in the face. Plus, I needed funds for tuition, and I didn't even have a car!

THE MIRACULOUS

When God gives a vision, however, He also gives provision. Once the Lord speaks and you capture His mind and begin to *"see as He sees,"* then you are able to achieve the impossible and attain the unattainable.

Spiritual insight carries you into the realm of the miraculous, and you begin to discover "nothing is impossible to them that believe." "Believe what?" you may ask. Believe God and that He has a purpose for your life.

15

That's what I did. I prayed fervently, "Lord, if you will help me in these areas, I will apply the rest of my life towards fulfilling the vision you have given me."

God's plan for my future came from the supernatural, certainly not from the circumstances that surrounded me. His blueprint for my life was set in motion before He knew me. Not because of my background and upbringing, but because the vision lined up with the Word of God.

For the first time I was tapping into God's sight, *not mine.* I was capturing the mind of God!

The Bible says, *"...he that hath begun a good work in you will perform it until the day of Jesus Christ"* (Philippians 1:6).

"GOOD NEWS"

After speaking with the college officials and telling them of my encounter with God, they agreed to allow me to return to school on probation. As we were discussing what that entailed, the dean said, "I see that you filled out a job application to work at the post office last year."

"Yes, sir," I replied. I was told that I was number fifty-seven on the waiting list and my chances of working there were slim to none since fifty-six other students were ahead of me. Plus, job turnover was minimal due to the great pay and benefits of working for the postal authority."

"Well, I have good news," the dean responded. "I've just received a phone call saying they need someone immediately. If you are willing to go to work right this minute the job is yours."

Hallelujah! I started work that day and God had provided the means to pay for my college tuition.

At the end of my first semester, amazingly, my grade point average was so high that I received a grant to pay for my schooling. My parents were so proud that they rewarded my hard work and diligence by purchasing a car for my use while in school. As for the draft, I never heard another word from Uncle Sam the entire time I was in college.

> *God's vision, once I embraced it, changed my circumstances so I could accomplish His will for my life.*

LIMITATIONS?

I can hear you saying, "This is easy for you to say, Pastor Rick. You have a big church and a worldwide ministry. Your family comes from a long line of pastors. Of course, everyone in your family hears from God. My family are just ordinary people. I am struggling to pay the bills and nobody knows who I am. Many of the things I have attempted have miserably failed. I don't think I've got what it takes to be successful."

You're mistaken! God is no respecter of persons! It is time to stop looking at your limitations. Begin to meditate on the Word and what the scriptures say pertaining to you. God says you are not to follow the masses. *"And be not conformed to this world: but be ye transformed by the renewing of your mind, that ye may prove what is that good, and acceptable, and perfect, will of God"* (Romans 12: 2).

There you have it! God says you can *know* His will!

IS IT POSSIBLE?

It is time to stop listening to self-defeating thoughts and words, and start realizing the mind is the battlefield. Your mind must be transformed in order to *"see as God sees."*

17

Start believing in the God of the miraculous and you can counteract those negative thoughts. You need to plant the Word in your mind so it can grow and be fertilized. By following the Father's principles, you can begin to believe all things are possible. *"I can do all things through Christ which strengtheneth me"* (Philippians 4:13).

God has never made, nor will He ever make, inferior human beings. You are created in His image and His likeness. Before any of your days existed the Bible says He knew you and ordained that you should be victorious. *"Beloved, I wish above all things that thou mayest prosper and be in health, even as thy soul prospereth"* (3 John 2 KJV).

You are not a mistake, an accident, or just one of the crowd.

You are uniquely created for the purpose of fulfilling a great destiny that God has ordained for your life. And here is the best part, the Lord already has a plan that assures your purpose and destiny will be a total success.

I didn't start at the place I am today. It is a fulfillment of what He promised.

STRUCK BLIND

Another man, in Biblical times, received his own bolt of lighting from God. The story unfolds in Acts 9: 1-31, where we are introduced to Saul who later becomes Paul, one of the most prolific writers of the Bible, as well as a staunch advocate of Jesus, after his conversion.

Before Paul's vision, he was a persecutor of Christians. He was a member of the Jewish sect called the Pharisees, and fiercely believed he was doing the will of God.

When Paul was struck down and blinded on the road to Damacus, he asked the same question many people ask at one time or another: "Lord, what do you want me to do?" Jesus gave him a command, "Now get up, go into the city and you will be told what you must do."

Blinded for three days, Paul had time to spend in earnest prayer. That is when God gave him a vision of a man, Ananias, who would come and lay hands on him. Ananias would restore his sight and speak to Paul about God's will for his life. You see, The Lord always has a plan!

God had also given Ananias a vision. The Lord called him to go and restore Paul's sight and to impart to him the infilling of the Holy Spirit. (Notice both men had to be in position and willing vessels for the vision to be accomplished.)

This was not an easy choice for Ananias because he knew who Paul was and what he had previously done to the followers of the "Way." But, God endowed Ananias with a supernatural confidence. He knew his assignment would not be impossible with the Lord on his side. Part of the vision that Ananias imparted to Paul was that he would become God's spiritual liaison between the Gentiles, the kings, and the Jewish people. Both men fulfilled their mission and the course of history was changed, forever!

CAPTURING HIS MIND

What about you? What is your God-imparted vision? Have you spoken with the Father and begun to *"see as He sees?"*

Perhaps there are plenty of reasons you don't think you see hope in your future. Could it be that you probably haven't understood the scripture concerning purpose, plan and destiny? After being born again you must work out your salvation with fear and trembling, believing that the Father has sent you here, just like the men of old, with divine purpose and destiny.

> ## *In order to capture the mind of Christ and "see as He sees," we must spend time with Him in prayer.*

That is when God can speak the secret things into our hearts and minds.

Perhaps you have never prayed this type of prayer. If not allow me to be your prayer partner. Let's offer these words together:

> *Father God, I come before You seeking Your purpose, plan, and destiny for my life. Forgive me Lord that I have not given You full reign or control over my life and circumstances. Lord, give me the vision You have prepared and let me see as You see. May I capture Your mind and work toward the vision all of my days. Strengthen and prepare me for Your will to be done.*
> *In Jesus' Name, Amen.*

Once you have heard His voice, it becomes a matter of decision and commitment. *"My sheep listen to my voice, I know them, and they follow me"* (John 10: 27 NIV).

YOU CAN BE HIS!

If at this point, you want to be sure you belong to God, that your name is written in the Lamb's Book of Life, now is the perfect time. Will you pray this prayer of salvation with me?

> *Father God, Today, I recognize that You love me that You sent Your Son, Jesus, to die on the cross for me. I ask You now to forgive my sins. I turn my back on sin. I receive You as my personal Savior. All that I am or ever hope to be, I give to You. Thank You Lord, that today I know I am a child of God.*
> *In Jesus' Name, Amen.*

If you spoke those words from the depths of your soul, let no one mislead you, you are one of His! Your sins have been washed in the precious blood of Jesus.

At this juncture, you must decide to do what God desires. Don't be tempted to turn to excuses.

THE WRONG MAN?

Moses, a mighty man of God, who the Lord called to lead the Israelites out of Egypt, had a long list of "But's."

The story is found in Exodus, chapters three and four. He tried to offer excuses to God explaining why the Lord must have picked the wrong man (even though he had been trained for this job from the time of his birth).

But, *"Who am I, that I should go unto Pharaoh, and that I should bring forth the children of Israel out of Egypt?"* (Exodus 3:11). Does this sound like something we might say given this assignment? Then God gives him the vision and reveals all He is going to do for him to prepare the way. Yet Moses is still not too happy with what he sees.

21

Again we hear "But" – "*But, behold, they will not believe me, nor hearken unto my voice: for they will say, The Lord hath not appeared unto thee*" (Exodus 4:1).

Have you ever heard someone around you comment, "What do you think you're doing?" or "Who do you think you are?"

NO MORE EXCUSES

Fortunately, God would have none of that behavior. He brushed aside Moses' excuses and began to confirm His words to him with miraculous signs that were intended to strengthen him and place fear into the enemy.

Once more we hear, "But." "*And Moses said unto the Lord, O my Lord, I am not eloquent, neither heretofore, nor since thou hast spoken unto thy servant: but I am slow of speech, and of a slow tongue*" (v.10).

This was startling considering the background of Moses. He was raised in the royal palace and studied under the best teachers and instructors. Moses knew in his spirit that he was destined for something great, but after all those years in Egypt, he had probably laid his dreams aside. The Lord spoke to him again saying, "*Who gave man his mouth? Who makes him deaf or mute? Who gives him sight or makes him blind? Is it not I, the Lord? Now go; I will help you speak and will teach you what to say*" (vv.11-12 NIV).

Moses had one more "but." He said, "*O Lord, please send someone else to do it*" (v.13 NIV). This sounds like so many people I have met.

THE CHALLENGE

Then God began to burn with anger! This is not a good situation for Moses or anyone else. Yet, the Lord is merciful and sends to Moses his brother Aaron, who is eloquent of speech so he can speak for him. All the bases are now covered, so what does Moses do? Does he rebel and run, or succumb to the superior force? Does he fulfill his destiny for himself, as well as others?

The vision God laid out for him brought Moses and the people of Israel (over 2 million) to their destiny and purpose. He was challenged by God to become the leader the Lord had originally intended him to be. God had shaped Moses and every circumstance to conform to His will.

> *When Moses captured God's mind he fulfilled his destiny, our destiny and God's will.*

Moses, step by step, began to piece the puzzle together – and God was faithful. The Lord sent the ten plagues and Pharaoh let the people go.

Because of one man's obedience, we have a story of incredible faith, the Ten Commandments, and how the Israelites were brought into the promised land – a land flowing with milk and honey.

Pause for a moment and reflect on what might have happened if Moses had let his past, his failures, and his shortcomings rule his future. What about *you?*

I would be less than truthful if I said I hadn't experienced turbulent times over the past 30 years. On the contrary, I've had many challenges and opportunities to quit and fail. In fact, there have been several times in my life and ministry where I felt justified in wanting to just give up. Each time these trials and tests came, however, the Lord would remind me of His vision for my life, and I was persuaded to carry on by His Spirit.

WHAT DETERMINES DESTINY?

The apostle Paul states in the book of Acts that he was actually *"...bound* [tied] *in the spirit"* (Acts 20:22). The apostle meant that his only choice was to do the will of God. As we have read previously, Paul had been given his assignment from God and during all those years he never lost his vision. He tells King Agrippa, *"...I was not disobedient unto the heavenly vision"* (Acts 26:19).

How does he explain keeping the vision? To the believers at Galatia he wrote, *"...I did not consult any man"* (Galatians 1:16 NIV). He did not confer with flesh and blood, but counseled with God by the Spirit.

Paul also declared, *"...I no longer live, but Christ lives in me"* (Galatians 2:20 NIV). It is the Lord's all sufficiency, thoughts, and voice we should be seeking for our destiny.

WHY TESTS AND TRIALS?

Have you ever stopped and considered that the reason you may be having so much trouble is because of the greatness of the *vision* God has for you? I know we can cause our own misery, but very few individuals I meet are trying to do that! The majority of the people I deal with are diligently searching for purpose and meaning in their life. Perhaps that is why things are so difficult for you right now. You may be closer to discovering your purpose and destiny than ever before, and the enemy is desperately trying to keep you from it.

Satan knows that if you and I fulfill God's vision for our lives, our destiny and purpose is going to be accomplished, and Satan's kingdom will suffer tremendously. So he works overtime sending "fiery trials" (temptations and tests) our way to discourage us. He realizes we are on the right track and are one stepping stone closer to achieving our completed objective!

The devil often knows more about our destiny and purpose than we can imagine. What a surprise Satan had at Calvary when Jesus defeated hell, death, and the grave.

The devil was not prepared for that. Satan thought he had actually killed the Son of God and won the battle between heaven and hell. Since that time, however, the enemy has doubled his efforts never to be surprised again – and he keeps his ear attuned to the prophetic voice of God. If he gets so much as an inkling that the Lord is going to use a certain person, place, or thing, he launches an attack to disable the vessel. Now that Satan and his minions cannot reach Jesus, they assault His followers.

Christ continues to suffer through His Body, the church. Jesus spoke to Saul, *"...why persecutest thou me?"* (Acts 9:4). When the enemies torment a Christian then they are really still persecuting Jesus.

You may ask, "Pastor, don't you think you are being rather melodramatic?"

No, not at all. Do you remember what happened when Jesus was born, and the devil became aware of the prophecy foretelling of the birth of a new "King"? What did he do? Not knowing which child it was, Satan inspired an edict to be issued demanding that every child two years old and under should be killed. The fact that his plot failed didn't discourage him in the least from continuing throughout Jesus' lifetime in attempting to destroy Christ and those He loved.

Satan's error was in not having all the pieces of the vision that the Father had planned for the Son. The devil thought that if he could just kill Jesus, then he had won. He never factored in the Resurrection.

Jesus came to give you an incredible life. *"The thief cometh not, but for to steal, and to kill, and to destroy: I am come that they might have life, and that they might have it more abundantly"* (John 10:10).

IMITATING THE ALMIGHTY

For a short time, Hitler ruled in glory, but his story ends with total devastation. That is how the devil works. He makes sin look good, smell good, and taste good. With cunning, he appeals to the carnal nature by making the situations in your life feel as though you couldn't be doing better. It is a lie that affects the lives of millions.

Satan attempts to imitate the Almighty, Omniscient, and Omnipotent God. As for Hitler, I wonder what his outcome would have been had he followed the Lord's path? One thing we know for sure, had he chosen God's plan, he would have spent his life in eternity with the Father. The Bible says, *"No man can serve two masters; for either he will hate the one and love the other; or else he will hold to the one and despise the other..."* (Luke 16:13).

God says, *"... choose you this day whom ye will serve"* (Joshua 24:15).

He declares, *"Behold, I set before you this day a blessing and a curse; A blessing, if you obey the commandments of the Lord your God, which I command you this day: And a curse, if ye will not obey the commandments of the Lord your God, but turn aside out of the way which I command you this day, to go after other gods, which ye have not known"* (Deuteronomy 11:26-28). Jesus said, *"...Ye cannot serve God and mammon"* (Matthew 6:24).

As for the saints of God, we are promised the blessings of heaven for serving Him. We belong to the family of our Abba Father and Jesus is our elder brother. As a result, we have a right to all the blessings of the family. We are to be blessed going in and coming out; in everything we set our hands to we will prosper, and our enemies will flee. This is victory in Christ.

THE CHOICE IS YOURS

God gives you a destiny full of hope, desire, goodness, mercy, and eternal life. He will bring into your life those strategies, concepts, and ideas that will allow you to capture His mind and see as He sees.

Each day purpose in your heart to make the right choice. Declare, *"...as for me and my house we will serve the Lord"* (Joshua 24:15).

When we follow God's principles of vision, nothing is impossible. In the next chapter we will discover how this applies to real life – from a cartoon character to one of the greatest dreamers of all time.

Never forget, vision makes the difference. It determines destiny.

He who belongs to God
hears what God says.
– John 8:47 NIV

CHAPTER 2

HOW TO
BE SUCCESSFUL
ALL THE TIME

*M*ickey and Minnie Mouse, Donald and Daisy Duck, Pluto and Goofy – do they sound familiar? They are names that always bring a smile or a giggle to any child, and most adults.

These cartoon characters are the result of the *vision* of an ordinary individual named Walt Disney. You say, "Ordinary?" Yes, Disney, born in Chicago, Illinois, and raised on a farm in Missouri, was simply a young man with a God-given artistic ability. He began his early years as an apprentice, doing commercial illustrations and cartoon art.

Seeking a more lucrative future, he journeyed to Hollywood to utilize his creative abilities. There, Disney found his first success with the creation of the cartoon character, Mickey Mouse. Eventually, his characters would find their way into advertising, publishing and franchising of goods.

Disney was a family man who was married to the same woman for forty-one years. Whenever he took his family to any type of amusement park, he would note the level of excitement and pleasure it brought to their faces. This began to give him the foresight to build the most successful amusement parks in the world: Disneyland, Los Angeles, CA., Walt Disney World, Orlando, FL., Disney Theme Park, Japan, and Euro-Disney.

He also established Los Angeles Art College, and produced numerous movies.

> *Walt Disney became one of the world's most extraordinary personalities by fulfilling his vision.*

At the time of his death, his empire was worth over one hundred million dollars per year.

Disney's success didn't occur overnight. He had to work his plan, step by step, and there was plenty of competition.

THANK GOD FOR VISIONARIES

Can you imagine the reaction when he told his family and friends of this new venture? Don't you think critics came crawling out of the woodwork? "Oh yeah, right! A theme park, and it's going to have what kind of characters walking around?" they must have asked.

Even his wife might have thought twice about this adventure. Perhaps she said, "Oh, yes, dear, let's take the family savings and start immediately!" He was proposing a project, which had no proven track record and was considered a risky business, at best. Wouldn't you love to know how Mr. Disney approached the bank with this concept? I sure would!

Many refer to people like Disney as "visionaries or

dreamers." Thank God for them.

THE DREAMER

One of the most provocative profiles of a Biblical "dreamer" is Joseph – better known as the man with the "coat of many colors."

Joseph was a young boy of seventeen as his story begins to unfold in the thirty-seventh chapter of Genesis. He was one of twelve sons and greatly favored by his father over the others. Sibling rivalry was already in the works long before he shared his vision with his brothers. So it didn't take much for his brothers to rise up in contempt and hate, after he told them his dream.

Obviously, that was a big mistake! He said to them, *"Listen to this dream I had: We were binding sheaves of grain out in the field when suddenly my sheaf rose and stood upright, while your sheaves gathered around mine and bowed down to it"* (Genesis 37:6-7 NIV).

Joseph's brothers became livid and their response was flavored with even greater hate. They asked, *"Do you intend to reign over us? Will you actually rule over us?"* (v.8).

HIS BROTHERS WERE SEETHING

If the situation wasn't already bad enough, Joseph had a second dream and again he shared this with his brothers – and this time with his father, Jacob. *"Listen,"* Joseph said, *"I had another dream, and this time the sun and moon and eleven stars were bowing down to me"* (v.9).

Jacob rebuked Joseph, just as his brothers had. He asked, *"What is this dream you had? Will your mother and I and your brothers actually come and bow down to the ground before you?"* (v.10).

31

His father kept the matter in mind, while his brothers were seething. Plotting how they would get rid of him, the brothers stripped him of the "coat of many colors," and threw him in a well to die. Joseph's brother, Rueben, had planned to return after the brothers had left him in the well, rescue Joseph and take him back to Jacob, but this attempt failed.

One of the other brothers, Judah, also did not want to kill him, so he conspired with his brothers to sell Joseph as a slave to the Ishmaelites. The brothers thought their schemes and plans had eliminated Joseph and his dream, forever. They had no way of knowing that his exile was only a prelude to Joseph's dream, as well as, their own destiny. God was already positioning Joseph – right where He wanted him.

QUESTIONING THE DREAM

The merchants sold the young Israelite as a slave to Potiphar in Egypt, one of Pharaoh's officials, the captain of the guard. There, Joseph excelled in his loyalty and duties and was highly esteemed by Potiphar.

There was only one problem. Potiphar's wife was angry because he had rebuffed her advances. He would always dash from the room, but this one time she grabbed his coat and took it to her husband. She claimed Joseph had left the coat behind after accosting her. Potiphar believed his wife, and, because of the alleged misdeed, Joseph was sent to the King's prison for several years.

At this point, Joseph must have begun to question his dream. Who wouldn't? The circumstances were certainly not indicative of the fulfillment of his vision. Despite Joseph's situation, however, he trusted God and remained faithful to what the Lord had shown him.

In prison, Joseph began to interpret the dreams of his fellow inmates, one who was the former baker to the Pharaoh

– and one who had been the chief butler to the king. Both the butler and baker had dreams that Joseph interpreted correctly. Eventually, the chief butler was restored to Pharaoh's confidence and the chief baker was beheaded.

After a few years, the chief butler remembered that Joseph had a talent for interpretation and summoned him to reveal Pharaoh's dreams. Joseph told Pharaoh he was to have seven years of plenty, to be followed by seven years of famine.

A ROYAL APPOINTMENT

Pharaoh was so impressed that he appointed Joseph as superintendent of the royal granaries. (Had Joseph not been placed in this position his vision could have never come to pass).

Joseph stored away grain for the lean years, and when his own brothers had no food for their families, the only place to receive provision was through the superintendent of the granaries. Well, what do you know! Fortunately, Joseph had not allowed his own feelings to spoil the big picture. He didn't harbor a grudge.

> *Joseph walked in forgiveness and fulfilled the destiny and purpose of himself and others.*

In this account we see the providence of God. Joseph told his family not to worry for the Lord had sent him ahead. *"And now, do not be distressed and do not be angry with yourselves for selling me here, because it was to save lives that God sent me ahead of you"* (Genesis 45: 5).

Joseph's story to this point is like opening Pandora's box,

each time you open the lid, unfortunate things begin to happen. Though you may be suffering through the most difficult time of your life, don't give up. As we see in the life of Joseph, there was good news around the corner. God brought healing and reconciliation to his family (Genesis 50:19).

COUNT IT ALL JOY

Just because circumstances do not appear to be in your favor does not mean that God is not in control. He *will* work things out for good for those who trust Him. The Word tells us, *"My brethren, count it all joy when ye fall into divers temptations; Knowing this, that the trying of your faith worketh patience. But let patience have her perfect work, that ye may be perfect and entire, wanting nothing"* (James 1:2-4).

Please note that it is *patience* that is being perfected, not our faith.

This scripture does not say to be joyful because you are in the fire, rather, it says to be joyful *in spite of* the fire. Why? Because the trying, or testing of your faith is going to produce something incredible in your life. It is called *patience* – which literally means "steadfastness or endurance."

No wonder Paul, writing to the Romans, exclaimed, *"And not only so, but we glory in tribulations also; knowing that tribulation worketh patience, and patience experience, and experience hope"* (Romans 5:3-4).

The word I want to draw your attention to is *"experience."* It means "tried integrity."

I don't know about you, but I am weary of listening to people who attempt to teach me how to live when they have never personally suffered. Dr. David Yongi Cho, Pastor of the world's largest church in Seoul, South Korea, states profoundly, "I don't trust anyone who walks without a limp."

Neither do I! If you want my respect, please show me your scars.

Don't try to say that life is not a struggle, and "If I'll just use my faith, I will never have a problem." The Bible doesn't teach that. Scripture declares that my faith will be tried and tested, but in so doing it will be refined into something far more useful and strong as I follow the Lord's *vision*.

The Word also declares that my integrity will become steadfast as I endure and overcome tribulations sent to discourage me. My joy is not in the trials themselves, rather in knowing that God will never fail me.

He will not allow me to fall if I just lean on Him and follow His direction.

Scripture tells us, *"Trust in the Lord with all your heart and lean not on your own understanding; in all your ways acknowledge Him. And He shall direct your paths"* (Proverbs 3:5-6 NIV).

We cannot control the actions of others, but we can control what our reactions will be.

It is also true that we cannot stop the tragedies of life, but we can learn to overcome every one of them through Jesus Christ, our Lord and Savior.

Don't allow misfortunes to compromise your vision and your destiny. Trust in the Lord and rest in His promises.

Planted deep within you is God's great purpose. Do not let Satan cheat you out of what is rightfully yours. Decide today that never again will you say, "I can't!" On the contrary, *you can!*

You were born to succeed and with God's vision, there is no stopping you. With Paul, you will say, *"I can do all things through Christ which strengtheneth me"* (Philippians 4:13).

NO LIMITS

On a mission trip to Thailand, I encountered a young man truly on fire for God, who was working his vision. I had been told that he was one of the translators and would be assisting me in the evening service. The only details I knew about him were that he came from the Aca tribe in the mountains and had started seven churches single-handedly. That sounded impressive to me.

He arrived on a small motorbike and took his place on the makeshift platform. During the service, I turned around and ask him to finish reading a scripture from the Bible; but instead he gave me a rather bemused look. No one had told me he couldn't read.

Immediately, the resident pastor informed me I would have to read on alone. You see, no one had ever said to the young man that because he couldn't read he would never do great and mighty works for God. No one had talked to him concerning limitations because of the color of his skin, or his lack of education. All he knew was that he was on fire for Jesus, and he moved into his destiny.

The most powerful thing a man can do is to become a visionary – to see what God sees.

THE POWER OF VISION

When the Lord gives you an insight into what lies ahead, everything about your life changes. Here are twelve ways we are transformed:

1. Vision is the key to our future and God's plan for our lives.

It enables us to escape both the bondage of the past and the snare of the present – and keeps us moving forward in destiny. Vision is a creative, productive force that allows us to go beyond the present and claim our future.

Never assume that just because things are difficult now they will always remain so. Realize that God has called us to be champions. If you are going to be the victor God has declared you to be, then you must do what it takes to triumph. As the cliché reminds us, "When the going gets tough, the tough get going!" Or, as the great visionary Winston Churchill once said, "Never, never, never give up!"

2. Vision makes us who we are.

The way you perceive yourself will determine the course of action you take regarding every aspect of your life. Vision equips you to perform and becomes the beacon of light that gives direction. It is what pulls you through the hard times, keeps you in the bad times, encourages you in the dry times, and causes you to carry on during the good times.

3. Vision controls our speech.

We are much more careful with our words when we know they are affecting our destiny. The Word of God declares, *"Death and life are in the power of the tongue; and they that love it shall eat the fruit thereof"* (Proverbs 18:21).

4. Vision determines our friendships.

We will not allow ourselves to become "unequally yoked" at any level of our lives when we know that our entire future is at stake. Godly friends believe in us – even when we question ourselves.

5. Vision controls our thoughts and decisions.

Every idea, concept, and strategy in our lives is influenced by the insight God has given us. We are not satisfied with the status quo, nor moved by the ideas of everyone else. The most popular thoughts of the day may not be the correct ones, and vision is what will keep us on course mentally.

6. Vision establishes our character.

It will cause us to become persons of great integrity. We will not do, nor *desire* to do, anything that could possibly interfere with God's plan. It is our vision that produces within us a commitment so strong that nothing the enemy does will deter or harm us. We obtain our identification from God, and realize, finally, "whose we are."

7. Vision will cause us to include others in our lives and plans.

The British writer, John Donne said, "No man is an island," and a person with heavenly insight understands this. I need you, and you need me. If we allow them to enter, mentors will come into our lives and elevate us. They will speak words of encouragement, and together we will build His Kingdom.

8. Vision creates motivation.

So you messed up! You feel like life has dealt you a bad hand. No big deal! If you keep focused on your dream, you will be motivated to go where you have never gone before – and accomplish what you have never done before.

9. Vision causes evaluation.

When you have a glimpse of your future, you suddenly have the ability to examine yourself and stay on course. That's how you finish the race you started.

Nobody desires failure, yet millions are guilty of quitting every day. Often it is because we do not correctly evaluate where we are headed and what we were doing. As a result, we become distracted and discouraged. Don't allow this to happen!

10. Vision causes transformation.

It gives us the ability to change into the person God wants us to become.

> *Many people fail simply because they are not flexible.*

One definition of insanity is "to do the same thing over and over again, expecting different results." It is just not going to happen. We need God's transformation. *"For my thoughts are not your thoughts, neither are your ways my ways, saith the Lord. For as the heavens are higher than the earth, so are my ways higher than your ways, and my thoughts than your thoughts"* (Isaiah 55: 8-9).

Our insights must be based on His thoughts, and His

ways, and that necessitates change. It means we must let go of the past and stop hanging on to the present. We cannot afford the mentality of "we've always done it this way."

> *Our vision must compel us to raise the bar and achieve all that God has designed for us.*

11. Vision creates dedication.

We should not be content with yesterday's triumphs, and miss today's opportunities. Vision causes us to "be all that we can be." Our commitment should be so dedicated to fulfilling our destiny, that to even contemplate failure would be totally out of the question.

12. Vision allows us to capture the mind of God.

When we begin to see as God sees, then we are able to dream the impossible, beat the unbeatable, think the unthinkable, do the unbelievable, and attain the unattainable. Of course, as surely as having a dream inspires us to press on toward total success in life, lack of *vision* ensures failure. It creates disunity, weariness, and a critical spirit, turns you into a faultfinder and destroys creativity.

A person lacking *vision* is constantly looking for someone or something to blame for their failures. That is why I believe with all my heart and soul that *the most powerful thing a person can do is to become a visionary and see what God sees.*

It is this ability which will ultimately identify, direct, and triumphantly carry us to the ultimate prize.

The Overcomers

We have been examining God's direction for your success, now let me give you a sure-fire recipe for failure: *Refuse to follow the vision God has for your life.*

If you want to guarantee that you will fail, just ignore the purpose God has revealed. If you refuse to press in and obtain His view of your future, you will never see His anointing released in and through you. The best you will be able to achieve is the "Burger King anointing" – you had it *your* way!

Is it possible to *always* succeed in life? Absolutely! Does that mean I will never experience temporary setbacks or run into obstacles? Of course not! Who wants to be around anyone who has never had to overcome a problem?

We must be people who learn from our mistakes, move forward, and become victorious. The apostle Paul admonished the church at Rome, *"...in all things we are more than conquerors through him that loved us"* (Romans 8:37).

Overcomers are filled with a vision for today and a burning passion for tomorrow. They will be the leaders of the 21st Century Church – on the cutting edge of all that is going to happen in this world. They will be the "success stories" that we read about, and many will become the movers and shakers who will set the course for this vital time in human history.

Overcomers will be the ones who will ultimately assist in ushering in the Second Coming of our Lord Jesus Christ. "How?" you ask. Because in fulfilling His *vision* for their lives, they will have helped pave the way for His eternal plan to be fulfilled. *"Now thanks be unto God, which always causeth us to triumph in Christ, and maketh manifest the savour of his knowledge by us in every place"* (2 Corinthians 2:14).

41

Is this your passion? If so, you will be successful *all* the time.

Dream the Impossible!
Beat the Unbeatable!
Think the Unthinkable!
Attain the Unatainable!

CHAPTER 3

PUTTING THE PIECES TOGETHER

Y ou may say, "Okay, Pastor Rick. You have shown me how vision determines my destiny, and that with God's insight I can be successful. I accept that. Plus, you mentioned how the process requires fitting the pieces of a puzzle together, but where do I begin?

It's a valid question, and we are ready to start.

The first definitive piece of the puzzle is determining whether the vision you have is "flesh birthed" or "spirit birthed." The Bible says, *"For to be carnally minded is death, but to be spiritually minded is life and peace"* (Romans 8: 6).

REAL LIFE

Do you recall the story of Nicodemus? He was a Pharisee, and a secret follower of Jesus. Speaking in the flesh, he asked the Lord, *"How can a man be born when he is old? can he enter the second time into his mother's womb, and be born?"* (John 3:4).

Jesus explained, *"That which is born of the flesh is flesh and that which is born of the Spirit is spirit"* (v.6). In other words, Jesus was teaching Nicodemus that in order to hear, think, and speak the will of the Father (not our own flesh) we must pass from mankind's spiritual death to spiritual life.

Paul wrote, *"And if Christ be in you, the body is dead because of sin; but the Spirit is life because of righteousness"* (Romans 8:10). He was able to declare, *"I am crucified with Christ: nevertheless I live, yet not I, but Christ liveth in me"* (Galatians 2:20).

FILLING THE VOID

The nature of physics states that where a vacuum exists, if allowed, air will come and fill it up. But even the Holy Spirit will not enter something that is already full. It is only when we have emptied ourselves of our will and submitted ourselves to the will of the Holy Spirit – accepting Jesus Christ as Savior – that the void is filled with the new birth. This is referred to as regeneration or re-creating.

How do you know if you have truly had this experience? Because the Bible says that, *"...old things are passed away; behold, all things are become new"* (2 Corinthians 5:17).

Father, Son and Holy Ghost have come and now dwell in the heart of the believer and we become united in spirit. *"But he that is joined unto the Lord is one spirit"* (1 Corinthians 6:17).

What we have actually done at this point is to place ourselves in a position where transition can occur. Through the new birth we become *ready* for the work of the Holy Spirit to lead and guide us into God's truth. *"And I will pray the Father, and he shall give you another Comforter, that he may abide with you for ever; Even the Spirit of truth; whom the world cannot receive, because it seeth him not, neither knoweth him: but ye now have him; for he dwelleth with you, and shall be in you"* (John 14: 16,17). The Holy Spirit not only teaches truth, but helps to promote within us the "fruit of the Spirit" – *"... love, joy, peace, longsuffering, gentleness, goodness, faith, meekness, temperance"* (Galatians 5:22-23).

Our spirit has now been placed in position, and we must begin to hear and receive from God. Scripture declares, *"The Spirit itself beareth witness with our spirit, that we are the children of God"* (Romans 8:16).

THE PRAYER FACTOR

As children of the Most High, the indispensable way we commune with God is through a dedicated, consistent prayer life. It is another important piece of the puzzle.

Prayer is considered the birthing canal of God.

We not only have the privilege of speaking with Him, but He speaks with us and we can begin to discern His will.

You will know the pieces are joining together if you are beginning to see as He sees, loving the things He loves, and despising the things He despises. When that transpires you will have the peace and assurance you are in God's perfect will.

This clarity helps us begin to view the things of the world from a different perspective. *"For who hath known the mind of the Lord, that he may instruct him? But we have the mind of Christ"* (1 Corinthians 2:16).

Rest assured that if we line up with the will of the Father; we find our own heart's desire.

45

THE BIRTHING PROCESS

As a youngster, I often heard great stories about the old time prayer warriors – how they travailed and went through what must have felt like *labor pains* in order to birth their prayer into the natural realm. Instead of audible words, *groaning* might have been all you heard during those prayer encounters. Yet, these warriors would not grow weary and leave until the task was completed.

This type of encounter closely relates to a burden – wrestling in prayer with a weighty issue. This is when we are able to feel a need in our heart before an event actually becomes reality.

Through prayer we can release this burden with the Holy Spirit's intercessory help. The Word says, *"Likewise the Spirit also helpeth our infirmities: for we know not what we should pray for as we ought; but the Spirit itself maketh intercession for us with groanings which cannot be uttered"* (Romans 8:26).

Birthing anything from the invisible into the visible will cause pain.

PRODUCTIVE PRAYER

Throughout scripture, we see the significance of "birthing prayers."

Elijah, the great prophet, said to Ahab, *"Go, eat and drink, for there is the sound of a heavy rain"* (1 Kings 18:41). So Ahab went off to eat and drink, *"but Elijah climbed to the top of Carmel, bent down to the ground and put his face between his knees"* (v.42). Can you visualize the birthing position?

The prophet said to his servant, "Go and look toward the sea." He went up, looked and said, "There is nothing there." Elijah knew what God was telling him, and repeated to the servant seven times, *"Go back"* (v.43).

The seventh time, the servant reported, *"A cloud as small as a man's hand is rising from the sea."* So Elijah said, *"Go and tell Ahab, 'Hitch up your chariot and go down before the rain stops you'"* (v.44).

Instantly, *"the sky grew black with clouds, the wind rose, a heavy rain came on and Ahab rode off to Jezreel"* (v.45).

This is the kind of prayer that James called a "fervent prayer." He wrote, *"The effectual fervent prayer of a righteous man availeth much"* (James 5:16).

James was talking about the power of the prophet's prayer. *"Elijah was a man just like us. He prayed earnestly that it would not rain, and it did not rain on the land for three and a half years. Again he prayed, and the heavens gave rain, and the earth produced its crops"* (James 5:17-18 NIV).

Elijah obviously spent time and energy, in birthing and burden, for his prayer to produce.

Paul expressed it this way: *"My little children, of whom I travail in birth again until Christ be formed in you,"* (Galatians 4:9).

BINDING AND LOOSING

It is evident that Father God requests our prayers in order to give life to His desires. If the Almighty was going to make this happen without the prayer of Elijah, then why didn't the prophet just stand idly by and wait to see what happened?

Jesus actually asks the disciples in Matthew 26:40, *"Could you not tarry one hour?"* In other words, He was asking, "You couldn't even spend one hour in prayer (in birthing and burden) with me?"

47

God goes so far as telling us to *command* Him. *"Thus saith the Lord, the Holy one of Israel, and his Maker, Ask me of the things to come concerning my sons, and concerning the work of my hands command ye me"* (Isaiah 45:11).

Yet, how can you issue a command if you don't even have a glimmer of the vision? Again the Lord says, *"Whatsoever ye shall bind on earth shall be bound in heaven: and whatsoever ye shall loose on earth shall be loosed in heaven"* (Matthew 18:18).

GOD'S WILL, NOT OURS

Just as with Elijah, and later with the disciples, there comes the understanding that God is asking for His children's participation regarding the events of things here on earth and in heaven. He requests the prayer of agreement. *"Again I say unto you, that if two of you shall agree on earth as touching anything that they shall ask it shall be done for them of my Father who is in heaven"* (v.19).

God calls us to pray with *"all prayer and supplication in the Spirit"* (Ephesians 6:8) – not with soul, or flesh prayers, but with seeking the Spirit-birthed vision for the will of the Father. This always produces unity, strength, truth, fruit, and creativity.

So often people make the mistake of setting goals before they pray, then try to find scriptures to validate those objectives. They don't seek God's direction, rather they pray to ask the Lord to bless what they are planning (flesh prayers).

Most of the time we can even find scripture, although out of context, to justify and help us stand rigid in our beliefs.

After thirty years in the ministry I have heard great success stories and incredible miracles resulting from prayer, as well as accounts that sounded more like "encounters of the third kind."

I'm not one to burst bubbles, but the goal is not to have God bless what we want blessed, rather to discover what He is blessing, and then parallel our vision and prayers with His. So that you become pliable in the Master's hands, I suggest you ask yourself a few pertinent questions:

- How much time have you spent in the Word, fasting, and praying?
- Are you a regular church-goer, or church-hopper?
- What is your motivation for the vision?
- Do you have a foundation for your faith?
- Will this vision enable you to live your life in such a way as to be a valuable witness for God?

ANGIE'S RESPONSE

A young woman named Angie Thomson, after a visit to Romania with her church family, returned home with an intense burden for the "Lost Children" of Romania. Stunned by the atrocities she had witnessed, her burden became indescribable. Angie, through much prayer, dared to respond to the call of her vision.

With great gusto, she returned to Romania and established shelters and clinics for hurting children. Angie became a beacon of light in a lost and torn world and is fulfilling the Great Commission.

Prayer is a remarkable tool for the success of our lives. It is what Father God has established as the direct communication between Himself and us. To many, however, prayer is something they know they should be practicing, yet they have doubts whether they will receive the desired results.

"QUE SERA, SERA"

There are countless Christians who don't even feel it is

necessary to pray. They believe because God is sovereign whatever is going to happen will happen, no matter what. They say, "Let life take it's natural course." And they agree with the song Doris Day made famous, "Que sera, sera, whatever will be will be. The future's not ours to see. Que sera, sera."

Amazingly, millions have believed this lie. People have even asked me, "Why should I pray? It doesn't seem to change what's happening."

What about you? Do you believe prayer and faith can alter a circumstance? I trust you will réad and meditate on the Word of God before you answer the question.

> *Has your prayer life taken on a "whatever" attitude, rather than an intimate time of relationship and communion with God.*

If you find yourself praying just because you feel you should – without any real belief answers will happen – you don't understand the power of prayer.

DON'T BE SURPRISED!

There are people in the Bible who were in a similar situation. The Book of Acts records a scene where many people gathered together to pray for the release of Peter, who had been put in jail. The angel of the Lord rescued Peter and he promptly journeyed to the house where the prayer meeting was in progress.

When Peter knocked on the door, a young woman was so

excited that she did not let him in. She ran to tell those who were praying and their reaction was amazing. *"'You're out of your mind,' they told her. When she kept insisting that it was so, they said, 'It must be his angel.' But Peter kept on knocking, and when they opened the door and saw him, they were astonished"* (Acts 12:15-16 NIV).

Did they think he was already dead? Why were they still praying if they thought that was true? People were still on their knees when the answer arrived.

Why the moment of surprise? Isn't this what they were praying for? Though they obviously didn't have the faith to believe their own prayer, God heard and answered. *"Lord, I believe; help thou mine unbelief"* (Mark 9:24).

YOUR SOURCE OF HOPE

Do you just want to stand idly by while your life is being altered through circumstances that you feel are out of your control? Perhaps your home is being foreclosed upon, your son or daughter is lost to drugs or dying of some incurable disease, or you've been given no hope for your own life. These are just a few of the many helpless situations we can find ourselves facing on a daily basis.

Did the God who created us abandon us without hope? Read the Word again. God declares He is bigger than our problems, and He cares. The Lord says, *"Come unto me, all ye that labour and are heavy laden, and I will give you rest. Take my yoke upon you, and learn of me; for I am meek and lowly in heart: and ye shall find rest unto your souls. For my yoke is easy, and my burden is light"* (Matthew 11:28-30).

He is Abba Father, the God who knows the exact number of hairs on your head. The God, who says, *"I will never leave thee, nor forsake thee"* (Hebrews 13:5). He is the God of the miraculous!

51

Does this sound like a Father who has left us with no hope? Why does He ask us the question, *"...Nevertheless when the son of man cometh, shall he find faith on the earth"* (Luke 18:8)? Is there no faith anywhere to produce prayers that effect change?

MOVING GOD'S HAND

The Spirit works in the realm of the supernatural, with prayers and faith as propellants. One of the most Spirit-filled individuals of our time was Smith Wigglesworth. Unschooled and a plumber by trade, Wigglesworth, conducted miracle faith services throughout the world, stirring the faith of thousands to receive healing and salvation. He stated, *"It is a luxury to be filled with the Spirit. I see everything a failure except that which is done in the Spirit."*

Wigglesworth was constantly led by the Holy Spirit, therefore, he was always in control of the situation facing him. He never ran from Satan; the devil ran from Him. He walked in this anointing because of prayer, faith, and holiness. The only anger he ever exhibited was against the devil.

Don't be deceived. The Word of God and prayer *does* move the hand of the Almighty. Read the story in Joshua chapter ten where God had the sun stand still because of prayer. We were not put here to fend for ourselves. Father God loved us so much that He gave His utmost. *"For God so loved the world, that he gave his only begotten Son, that whosoever believeth in him should not perish, but have everlasting life"* (John 3:16).

MAKE THE CALL

Would you like to know God's personal telephone number? He invented voice dialing long before the cellphone.

The Lord says, *"Call unto me, and I will answer thee, and shew thee great and mighty things, which thou knowest not"* (Jeremiah 33:3).

Speak to Him and see how quickly He responds. Like any good parent, He will be delighted to hear from you!

Our Heavenly Father (Abba) calls us to be ambassadors – His representatives, just as the disciples were. As with the disciples on the Day of Pentecost (Acts 2:4), we are given the baptism in the Holy Ghost with the evidence of a heavenly language. This was imparted to endue us with power from above, and we are expected to operate with that same unction and anointing today.

THE PROMISE

Before Christ ascended to heaven, He declared, *"And, behold, I send the promise of my Father upon you: but tarry ye in the city of Jerusalem, until ye be endued with power from on high"* (Luke 24:49). With this anointing we can tie the hands of the enemy in prayer.

Our transformation through the Holy Spirit has positioned us to speak the Word; opposing the works of the devil and bringing restoration to a lost and dying world. We are told to, *"Heal the sick, cleanse the lepers, raise the dead, cast out devils: freely ye have received, freely give"* (Matthew 10: 8).

Just as the disciples declared, we should be able to repeat, *"...Lord, even the devils are subject unto us through thy name"* (Luke 17:10).

Amazing things are taking place. In the past few decades we have witnessed millions in the nation of Korea convert from oriental religions to Christianity. Much of this is attributed to the over 800,000 actively involved members of the church pastored by Dr. David Yongi Cho.

Dr. Cho has used the example of the model prayer found

53

in Matthew, as a pattern to follow. Cho believes in "praying and obeying." Not only has a country been changed, but countless churches have been birthed from the outline of this prayer.

THE LORD'S PRAYER

There are many types of prayer – such as one of dedication, thanksgiving, praise, intercession and petition. Jesus, however, left us a model prayer by which He was always prepared for whatever situations were taking place in His life. You can use it, too.

Let us look at the Lord's Prayer in Matthew 6: 9-13, as well as the attributes of His Name.

After this manner therefore pray ye:

Our Father which art in heaven, Hallowed be thy name (God is being magnified).
> Sin: Jehovah-Tsidkenu - Jehovah our Righteousness
> Jehovah-Mkaddesh - Jehovah who Sanctifies

Thy kingdom come. Thy will be done in earth, as it is in heaven.(Guidance and divine understanding).
> Spirit: Jehovah-Shalom - Jehovah Is Peace
> Jehovah-Shammah - Jehovah Is There

Give us this day our daily bread (Bread - provision).
> Soundness: Jehovah-Jireh - Jehovah My Provider
> Jehovah Rophe - Jehovah Heals

And forgive us our debts as we forgive our debtors
(For ourselves, others, and obligations).
    Success: *Jehovah-Nissi - Jehovah My Banner*

And lead us not into temptation, but deliver us from
evil: For thine is the kingdom, and the power, and
the glory, for ever. Amen.
    Security: *Jehovah-Rohi - Jehovah My Shepherd*

Jesus is the only way we can approach the Father, and through His Name we have power and authority.

Obviously, God meant for us to spend time in prayer, otherwise why were we given this example which covers every area of our lives: *sin, spirit, soundness, success, and security*? Why would He ask for His will to be done on earth as it is in heaven? How did He plan to have His will accomplished? It is most certainly through the people of God and prayer.

BY THE BOOK

The Lord calls on us to meditate on His Word – another essential aspect of the puzzle. *"This book of the law shall not depart out of thy mouth; but thou shalt meditate therein day and night..."* (Joshua 1:8). By obeying, we are allowing scripture to paint on the canvas of our minds and hearts the picture of our destiny.

When we have received the revelation of God's Word, though our prayer and meditation, the Father gives us ideas, concepts and strategies to bring about His vision in our life. *"Open thus mine eyes, that I may behold wondrous things out*

55

of thy law." (Psalm 119:18).

IT'S QUICK AND POWERFUL

One principle is clear: *you cannot meditate on what you have not taken in!* Jesus declared, *"...Man shall not live by bread alone, but by every word that proceedeth out of the mouth of God"* (Matthew 4:4).

As we have discovered, prayer builds our spirit man, but it is the Word of God that trains and illuminates our minds. You must, *"Study to shew thyself approved unto God, a workman that needeth not to be ashamed, rightly dividing the word of truth"* (2 Timothy. 2:15). *"For the word of God is quick, and powerful, and sharper than any twoedged sword, piercing even to the dividing asunder of soul and spirit, and of the joints and marrow, and is a discerner of the thoughts and intents of the heart"* (Hebrews 4:12).

CARNAL CHRISTIANS?

The apostle Paul tells us, *"But the natural man receiveth not the things of the Spirit of God: for they are foolishness unto him: neither can he know them, because they are spiritually discerned"* (1 Corinthians 2:14).

Why can't the "natural man" comprehend the things of God? Scripture says the Spirit gave the apostles the words:
"...but holy men of God spake as they were moved by the Holy Ghost" (2 Peter 1:21).

Only after conversion do we have the Spirit of God dwelling in our mortal bodies; thus we can have spiritual discernment and begin to understand spiritual knowledge. Paul spoke to the church in Corinth concerning the difference between a carnal Christian and a spiritual Christian. He said, *"For ye are yet carnal..."* (1 Corinthians. 3:3).

Paul was obviously frustrated at their lack of spiritual development. They were still clinging to the philosophies of the world – causing strife and division among themselves, still full of pride and not living by Godly standards.

The Corinthians were spiritual babies, working through the flesh instead of renewing their minds in the Word.

A REVELATION

How can we grow from infancy into spiritual maturity? Spend time with the Lord.

Rather than hurrying through your prayer life and God's Word, schedule the time into your daily agenda and keep that commitment faithfully – as you would any other important matter. You will be pleased with the results.

God's impartation of revelation guarantees manifestation. That is why I daily devote a minimum of thirty minutes strictly to seeking and meditating on His Word.

In the words of the psalmist, *"The meek will he guide in judgment; and the meek will he teach his way"* (Psalm 25:9). What you receive in your prayer time with the Lord, will immediately begin to work on your behalf, as you follow His voice. Why? Because what begins in the spiritual, is transformed into the physical.

> *You must first have a*
> *spiritual reality before you can*
> *have a true physical reality.*

If the flesh is dominating the spirit, you have only created a guise, and you are destined for sorrow. Pay attention to these words, *"And he gave them their request; but sent leanness into their soul"* (Psalm 106:15).

Once, the Israelites asked the prophet Samuel if they could replace him with a King after his death. The Lord heard the conversation and gave them their request with a warning. God said to Samuel, "*... it is not you they have rejected, but they have rejected me as their King"* (1 Samuel 8:7). And the Lord added, "*...show them the manner of the king that shall reign over them"* (1 Samuel 8:9).

Yet, even with all the warnings and God's will not being fulfilled, they chose their own path. In the end, however, they were crying out to God for relief from their king.

CHILDREN OF PROMISE

The flesh and the spirit have always been in conflict.

Abraham had two sons, one who was conceived by the spirit the other by the flesh (in the ordinary way, not by the power of God). In Genesis 16 we read that Abraham was given the promise by God to make him the Father of many nations through a son. But as time went by and Abraham was getting older, he didn't see any signs of this fulfillment.

In haste, he and his wife, Sarah, decided to help God. In the flesh, they recruited the maidservant (Hagar), who produced a son (Ishamael). This, of course, was not the son given by the power of the Spirit, and it brought them nothing but problems and heartache. Without fervent prayer to accomplish our Spirit-birthed vision, we too are susceptible to life-long ramifications from our decisions of flesh.

Centuries later Paul wrote, *"Now we, brethren, as Isaac was, are the children of promise. But as then he that was born after the flesh persecuted him that was born after the Spirit, even so it is now"* (Galatians 4:28-29).

YOUR DECISION

You may feel you hear clearly from the Lord, but remember: *God will not force you to follow His voice or His plan.* This is your free-will decision based on the principles He established from the creation of the universe.

In addition to the flesh, there may be other conditions holding you back from God's desired destiny. Satan is looming in the background. There is a reason the Lord's Prayer includes the words, *"deliver us from evil."*

Satan prowls as a roaring lion, seeking whom he may devour. He will cause your flesh and soul to birth your vision out of personal desire or need. This is not a true Spirit-birthed prayer. Let me warn you that "need" will only produce a vision based on *fear, anger, rejection or crisis.*

A vision birthed in the natural – by need – is temporal. One birthed by the Spirit is eternal.

REMOVING THE FEAR

It's time to realize that fear is an emotion that has the potential to create vision – even if it is the wrong kind. According to Webster's dictionary, *"fear is the painful emotion of impending danger."* It's a powerful motivating force.

During my years of counseling, I have encountered numerous people who destroyed their lives by operating out of the spirit of fear, rather than the spirit of faith.

- "I'm afraid I am going to die of cancer, because it runs in our family."
- "I just know I am going to be a failure, because my father and grandfather were never successful!"

- "I'm afraid I'm going to lose my spouse because I'm getting old and out of shape!"

Fear can absolutely decimate your destiny and vision. Job complained, *"What I feared has come upon me; what I dreaded has happened to me"* (Job 3:25, NIV).

If you see yourself as a failure, you *will* be a failure. Remember, *the me I see is the me I'll be.*

Learn to grow from your mistakes. The Bible declares, *"For God hath not given us the spirit of fear; but of power, and of love, and of a sound mind..."* (2 Timothy 1:7).

Another type of anxiety is the fear of people. Do not permit the needs of others to control your future. It will guarantee failure for you and destroy God's direction for your life. When you examine the New Testament, you find that Jesus was never moved by the needs of all the people. He would walk into situations and heal only one person while others who needed His touch did not receive a miracle that day. Why? Because He based everything He did on what the Father said. He loved the people, but He served only God.

TURNING FEAR TO RESPECT

In Israel, Saul was given a direct command by God to do a certain deed. He compromised what the Lord told him to do and said, *"I was afraid of the people and so I gave in to them"* (1 Samuel 15:24). Ultimately, this cost Saul his position as King of Israel. God sought one who was *"after mine own heart"* (Acts 13:22).

Be certain of this: you will never accomplish His purpose as long as you worry about what people say concerning you and yield to their demands. You must set your mind on things above and stay spiritually focused.

God never motivates His people by frightening them.

While we are admonished to "fear the Lord," this has nothing to do with the *spirit* of fear described by Paul to young Timothy.

Fearing God has to do with honoring Him as King and Lord of our lives. I respect Him to the degree that I would never knowingly rebel against Him. My fear (respect) of Him motivates me to seek Him, serve Him, and worship Him with my whole heart.

I am not afraid of God. I am in love with Him and honor Him with the esteem and respect He deserves.

No More Anger

The emotion of anger can create vision – but the wrong kind.

Moses once smote a rock to get water because the pressure was on him to do something *now* (Numbers 20:7-12). Instead of obeying what he knew to be the will of God, he allowed his anger to move him in a direction the Lord never intended.

If you are not careful, your wrath will turn to vengeance and you will find yourself consumed with thoughts of getting even.

It is impossible to hear and receive from God when you are devoured by pent up emotions. Your mind immediately starts to play the, "Another Somebody Done Somebody Wrong Song."

You may be harboring bitterness because you lost your parents to divorce or death. Perhaps there is a torn relationship between you and your Christian brother or sister. Maybe you even have anger toward God for what you feel are prayers left unanswered. Stop, and ask the Lord to redirect your thoughts.

HIS WAY

The Lord calls us to walk in forgiveness – not because we feel that way, but because we choose His way over ours. The Word says, *"...let not the sun go down upon your wrath"* (Ephesians 4:26).

Learn to separate the person from the evil spirit working through them or around them. In prayer give your burdens to the Lord. I love the words of Jesus, *"For my yoke is easy, and my burden is light"* (Matthew 11:30).

> *Let your mind be centered on Christ. Don't allow it to wander on fantasies or dwell on revenge.*

Otherwise you will gradually be worn by the wiles of the devil. *"For we wrestle not against flesh and blood, but against principalities, against powers, against the rulers of the darkness of this world, against spiritual wickedness in high places"* (Ephesians 6: 12).

SHOWER THEM WITH LOVE

Paul once preached in Macedonia where a "spirit of divination" was working through a certain woman. She followed after him, shouting, *"These men are servants of the Most High God, who are telling you the way to be saved"* (Acts 16:17 NIV).

She continued these outbursts for several days. Finally, Paul became so troubled that he turned around and said to the spirit, *"I command thee in the name of Jesus Christ to come out of her. And he came out the same hour"* (Acts 16:18).

Notice, "he" is used to acknowledge the evil spirit, and Paul treated the woman in the third person. He separated her from the evil spirit.

When people cause you pain or anger, and you are tempted to turn your back on them, learn to target the real enemy. Be angry at the devil not the person. Like Paul, instead of shutting them out of your life, rebuke the spirit and then begin to shower them with love and walk in forgiveness. Despise Satan and hurl your wrath at him. That is how your anger can become your power.

Learn to resist your enemy by taking *"...unto you the whole armor of God, that ye may be able to withstand in the evil day, and having done all, to stand"* (Ephesians 6:13).

It was just after casting the evil spirit out of the fortune-teller, that Paul and Silas were beaten, arrested and thrown in prison. The woman's masters saw their future financial gains dwindling!

Then came midnight! That is the hour when Paul and Silas prayed and sang praises unto God. The earth shook the foundation of the prison and immediately all the doors were opened, and the shackles of every prisoner were broken.

DRASTIC ACTION

There is a wonderful song we sing in our church that includes these words: *"Shake off those heavy bands, lift up those holy hands."*

Regardless of the situation, no matter how hopeless it looks, if you are right with God, begin to praise Him and watch those chains fall off.

You may even face an obstacle so severe that drastic action is need. Facing one demon, Jesus said, *"This kind can come forth by nothing, but by prayer and fasting"* (Mark 9:29).

63

That is what Daniel did. He said, *"And I set my face unto the Lord God, to seek by prayer and supplications, with fasting, and sackcloth, and ashes"* (Daniel 9:3).

God heard that prayer. He declared, *"Fear not, Daniel: for from the first day that thou didst set thine heart to understand, and to chasten thyself before thy God, thy words were heard, and I am come for thy words"* (Daniel 10:12).

A NATIONAL FAST

Derek Prince, in his book, *Shaping History Through Prayer and Fasting,* recalls a story about a fast proclaimed by Abraham Lincoln. The president called for three separate days of national humiliation, prayer and fasting. The reason for each of these was the Civil War, and the central theme of the petition was for the restoration of national peace and unity.

Lincoln's first proclamation was requested by a joint committee of both Houses of Congress, and the day was set apart for the last Thursday in September, 1861. Here is a paraphrase of that request.

> *That this prayer would be offered with fervent supplications to almighty God for the safety and welfare of these States, His blessing on their arms and a speedy restoration of peace. And, whereas it is fit and becoming in all people, at all times, to acknowledge and revere the Supreme Government of God; to bow in humble submission to his chastisements; to confess and deplore their sins and transgressions, in the full conviction that the fear of the Lord is the beginning of wisdom, and to pray for the pardon of their past offenses, and for a blessing upon the present*

and prospective actions.
    – Appendix no. 7&8, Volume 12,13
    U.S. Statues At Large

From the beginning of the seventeenth century until at least the second half of the nineteenth century, public days of prayer and fasting played a vital and continuing role in shaping the national destiny of the United States. This event occurred over 140 years ago, yet we have to ask ourselves how much of the blessings and privileges we now enjoy were obtained for us by the prayers of our leaders and governments in previous generations?

A WAKE-UP CALL

Throughout history, as people fall away from His commandments and make their own rules and regulations, they ultimately fall to their knees, begging God for mercy from the evil penetrating their lives.

We were all shocked at the shattering events of September 11, 2001. When the World Trade Towers and part of the Pentagon in our nation's capitol were hit by terrorists, global headlines blared, "America Under Attack."

Millions were glued to their televison sets watching in disbelief and horror as the story unfolded with the loss of thousands of lives. An assault of this magnitude had never happened before in the United States.

Like Lincoln, the response of President George W. Bush was to rally the country in prayer and a recognition of a dependency upon our Heavenly Father. Members of Congress stood together on the Capitol steps and sang "God Bless America" – a scene that will be indelibly etched in our memory.

We have had a wake-up call, and must forever remember we live in a dispensation of grace and mercy.

Oh, that we will heed the words of God when He cried, *"If my people, which are called by my name, shall humble themselves, and pray, and seek my face, and turn from their wicked ways; then will I hear from heaven, and will forgive their sin, and will heal their land"* (2 Chronicles 7:14).

How do we put the pieces together? Our vision is made clear through prayer and the Word, but must be grounded in something eternal – the Spirit of God. *"While we look not at the things which are seen but at the things which are not seen: for the things which are seen are temporal; but the things which are not seen are eternal"* (2 Corinthians 4:18).

With this foundation, we are ready to examine a topic we cannot escape – change!

CHAPTER 4

CHANGE YOUR DESTINY

W hat if God simply *crystallized* you where you are right now – not allowing you to make any changes for the rest of your life? Think how strange it would feel if you were frozen in time!

Perhaps you are a status-quo kind of person who prefers to keep things just the way they are. You fear change or upheaval of any kind. I have had people in my own congregation tell me, "Oh, Pastor, let's just stay the way we are, we don't need to grow." You can probably guess my reaction to that brilliant idea!

Let us pretend for a moment you have just experienced the worst day you can ever remember. To make matters worse, you awaken the next morning, and the next, to repeat the routine again and again. This daily drudgery continues for what seems like an eternity until you can't take it another minute. What are your choices?

1. Keep repeating the day until your life is over.

2. Remain in the status-quo and weather the storm until you are too old and tired to care.
3. Challenge yourself to start making changes.

What is it going to be? I pray you choose the third option.

Let me recommend that you watch the movie, *Groundhog Day* – perhaps a few times. It will give you a visual concept of finding purpose in life. The film shows how change can come about in the natural, so just imagine what can be done with Christ working in you.

Later in this chapter we will explore the spiritual dynamics of the decisions you make.

OPEN THE DOOR

You can revolutionize your life and destiny by being willing to accept ideas that bring about *change*. When transformation begins, you have opened the door for miracles to enter.

Have you ever considered the possibility that your attitude or way of thinking is preventing your miracle from happening? If you are the type of person who looks toward the future, this is the time to pause and meditate on the word *change* – a crucial piece of the puzzle.

The dictionary defines "change" as: *to cause to become different, alter, transform, or convert.*

One of the most quoted scriptures on this topic is found in Romans 12:2: *"And be not conformed to this world: but be ye transformed by the renewing of your mind, that ye may prove what is that good, and acceptable, and perfect, will of God."*

This verse makes it abundantly clear that we cannot afford to remain the same! If you hold on to the idyllic notion that you can progress without transformation, you will never walk in the good, acceptable, and perfect will of God. This should be our greatest desire. The Lord is telling us through His Word exactly how to go about making a move for the better – by the *renewing of the mind!*

TOTAL SURRENDER

The moment we accept Jesus (our first change), the Holy Spirit comes to dwell in us and begins to open our eyes to spiritual truth. After this initial step, however, many have a problem. It is wonderful to have Jesus as our Savior, but another story to have Him as Lord. This is where a power struggle often takes place and we sense a reluctance to forfeit full control over our minds, our lives and our circumstances.

For a "doubting Thomas" who is not sure that total surrender is the right path to take, read what took place in the life of Cain (Genesis 4:11). Better yet, continue the story and learn what happened to Seth, his brother, Abel's replacement. Seth's family begins to acknowledge and call upon the name of the Lord in every situation. What a difference it makes!

THE METAMORPHOSIS

When we are willing to accept Jesus as both Savior and Lord, we begin the process of transformation – or what could be referred to as *metamorphosis.* These words are similar by definition.

Transformation means a marked change in appearance and character.

In biology, metamorphosis is in the form (and often the habits) of an animal during normal development after the embryonic stage. Picture a caterpillar – a worm – that has

69

been in the cocoon, only to break out and take on the trappings of a beautiful and stunning butterfly.

I am not comparing you to a worm, rather a human being. As the psalmist wrote, *"...the earth is full of your creatures"* (Psalm 104:24 NIV). The word *creature,* "something created," is used to refer to those designed by God in *His* image. It also means *one dependent on or subservient to another.* Dependency upon God was established from the beginning of time.

After our embryonic stage, we too begin to break out of the cocoon of old patterns, habits and thoughts. The renewing of our mind causes us to perceive spiritual words as truth. Jesus declares, *"Neither do men put new wine into old bottles: else the bottles break, and the wine runneth out, and the bottles perish: but they put new wine into new bottles, and both are preserved"* (Matthew 9:17). We need to become fresh wine!

LIKE AN EAGLE

In the book, *Restoring the Christian Family,* John and Paula Sandford tell the story of the development of the eagle, one of God's amazing creations. Approximately every seven years, an eagle must renew itself. Its wing feathers become brittle, and laden with oil and dirt.

The mighty eagle retires to a cave or hiding place high above the reach of predators. There he begins the arduous process of renewal. With his great beak he plucks out the wing feathers one by one. Next, each talon is removed, claw by claw, until the bird is defenseless – except for his beak which he proceeds to smash against the rocks until it too is broken off. Patiently the bird waits until his feathers, talons and beak are renewed.

The old eagle is gone, and a new version emerges. The transformation is complete.

Old feathers represent old insights and failures. By removing the past, we allow the new to spring forth.

As an eagle, we can fly high and have great vision.

I am not implying we have to retreat to a cave and start clawing, yet in order for God to do a mighty work and refine us as gold, we must begin to live by His words. The Bible declares, *"All scripture is given by inspiration of God, and is profitable for doctrine, for reproof, for correction, for instruction in righteousness"* (2 Timothy 3:16). *"For whom the Lord loveth he correcteth; even as a father the son in whom he delighteth"* (Proverbs 3:12).

In Hebrews we read, *"...My son, despise not thou the chastening of the Lord, nor faint when thou art rebuked of him: For whom the Lord loveth he chasteneth, and scourgeth every son whom he receiveth. If ye endure chastening, God dealeth with you as with sons; for what son is he whom the father chasteneth not?"* (Hebrews 12:5-7).

The Christian is born anew. *"Which were born, not of blood, nor of the will of the flesh, nor of the will of man, but of God"* (John 1:13).

EMBRACE CHANGE

The Lord is not content to pat us on the back and let us relax just because we made our first initial change. His goal is to stretch us, cutting and pruning anything that does not bear fruit. We are assured, *"He who hath begun a good work in us will complete it until the day of Jesus Christ"* (Philippians 1:6).

God will not allow us to wallow in the plight or our past, nor to become complacent in the present. His desire is that we fulfill our mission. As we have read, to accomplish this means we must renew our way of thinking.

Change can never take place when a person continues to do the same thing in the same way and expects a different result.

We must *embrace* what is new and fresh in order to grow in Christ!

BRANDED ON YOUR MIND

The Word declares that the mind needs renewing. Why? It is because the reservoir of our thoughts can hold onto old strongholds and mindsets that hinder us from changing our destiny.

How are these patterns created? Here is one example: Suppose you are a toddler and you don't yet understand the potential dangers lurking around you. In the kitchen you are alone for a moment when you decide to touch the fascinating red glow on the stove. At that instant, your mother walks in and screams, "Don't touch that!"

You cry, she screams, and the memory is forever branded on your mind. Through such an experience, a mindset has been established. For a lifetime you will always remember both the physical reaction of the pain, and the sound of your mother's panic-stricken voice. You have been programmed.

DISCOVERING TRUTH

Here is another example. For centuries people believed the world was flat and sailors wouldn't even consider crossing the ocean because of this superstition. History tells us they were fearful of dropping off the edge of the earth if they traveled too far.

Nevertheless, because of new information indicating otherwise, a few brave souls ventured out and discovered the truth. They found the earth was actually round – and life changed drastically for mankind. What is the point? All strongholds must be replaced by truth.

As we read and study scripture, the scales begin to fall from our eyes. We gradually replace erected strongholds with the Word of God, which is all truth. This is why when we first come to God we are considered infants. *"As newborn babes, desire the sincere milk of the word, that ye may grow thereby"* (1 Peter 2:2).

Meanwhile, the spiritually mature have broken down these barriers and are feeding on solid food. *"Anyone who lives on milk being still an infant, is not acquainted with the teaching about righteousness. But solid food is for the mature, who by constant use have trained themselves to distinguish good from evil"* (Hebrews 5: 13-14 NIV).

TIME TO REPROGRAM

The Word is what bypasses our mistaken beliefs. *"For the word of God is quick, and powerful, and sharper than any two-edged sword, piercing even to the dividing asunder of soul and spirit, and of the joints and marrow, and is a discerner of the thoughts and intents of the heart"* (Hebrews 4:12).

Our emotions and thoughts can feel so comfortable and normal that it keeps us confined to the present. Without a new understanding, we could easily depreciate our true value to the Kingdom of God.

Just as a computer, we often need reprogramming.

Jesus told a parable depicting the state we are in before conversion – and sometimes even afterwards. He said, *"Verily, verily, I say unto you, Except a corn of wheat fall into the ground and die, it abideth alone: but if it die, it bringeth forth much fruit. He that loveth his life shall lose it; and he that hateth his life in this world shall keep it unto life eternal"* (John 12: 24, 25).

If there is no dying to our habits, attitudes and belief systems, how can the Word empty the old and refill us with the new?

Unless we fill this void in our spirit with truth, we will never be set free. There will be no change or growth.

ARE YOU WILLING?

King Saul, the predecessor of King David, had a chance to lead according to the Father's plan. However, as we read in 1 Samuel chapter sixteen, his willful personality and his own desires caused him to miss out on the blessings of God.

Saul was God's first choice, but he would not accept the

words of obedience; he always had to insert himself into the picture. The Lord was so displeased that His Spirit departed from Saul and was given to David.

What was the difference between the two men? King David's brokenness and willingness to change brought repentance. He had a heart for God.

Why should our walk with the Lord be any different than King David or one of the original disciples? After all, these are our examples of how to go forth in the name of Jesus and walk in freedom – teaching, and preaching the Gospel.

After their conversion to Christ, the disciples gave up their homes, friends and family. *"And anyone who does not take his cross and follow me is not worthy of me"* (Matthew 10:38 NIV). One disciple was told he would not even be allowed to go back and bury his father (read Luke 9:59-60).

Before bearing the kind of fruit Jesus expected, total commitment was required. Prior to going out into the highways and byways, the chosen twelve spent time with Jesus – following in His footsteps, learning from the Master.

THE DECISION

The prophet Isaiah is another servant of God who understood the necessity of change. He gives us insight into this concept when he made the decision to stop dwelling on the past and to refrain from leaning on what was old and familiar. God told him, *"Remember ye not the former things, neither consider the things of old, Behold, I will do a new thing; now it shall spring forth; shall ye not know it? I will even make a way in the wilderness, and rivers in the desert"* (Isaiah 43:18-19).

Because we were given freedom of choice from the very beginning, it is still up to us to make decisions concerning the issues of life. However, as you have read, there are spiritual dynamics that need to be implemented when choosing options.

Change is wrapped up in the word *decision*. A choice must be made whether you decide to be:

- Bound to the present.
- Discouraged by the past.
- Seeking God's vision and moving forward toward your objective.

Let your controlling influence be the excitement and anticipation of where you are going, not where you have been. As Paul said, *"...Forgetting what is behind and straining toward what is ahead."* (Philippians 3:13 NIV).

LESSONS FROM LEPERS

Both Isaiah and Paul are saying, "If you want to move on with your life and succeed, then stop hesitating and looking over your shoulder. Make a firm decision to go forward in faith!"

That is exactly what the four lepers did in the Old Testament. Scripture records, *"Now there were four men with leprosy at the entrance of the city gate. They said to each other, 'Why stay here until we die? If we say, "We'll go into the city" – the famine is there, and we will die. And if we stay here, we will die. So let's go over to the camp of the Arameans and surrender. If they spare us, we live; if they kill us, then we die.'"* (2 Kings 7:3-4 NIV).

They made a decision *not to be bound to the present*, but to alter their circumstances and take a chance that would forever change their future.

These men had a huge dilemma. Not only were they lepers and outcasts from society, they were living in a time of famine when Samaria was being persecuted by Syria.

The Word of the Lord had come forth from Samaria; but because of the turmoil around them, the people were unable to receive or believe what God said. So the Lord used the four lepers. Without even being aware of it, God moved them into their destiny and allowed them to be the vehicle whereby He freed Samaria.

Had they been discouraged by their predicament, they would have never walked into their miracle. Without question, something extraordinary took place for these lepers, but they participated in the process:

1. They faced their fear.

Being considered the dregs of society there were strict rules that regulated what these lepers could and could not do. To break such rules often meant certain death. However, they came to the realization that if they stayed where they were, the future was hopeless. This brought them to the conclusion, *"Why sit here until we die?"*

Recognizing the bottom line of what could happen, they faced their fear, stepped out and believed that something greater was ahead for them.

2. They took responsibility for themselves.

You can never move ahead in life if you are constantly blaming some*one* or some*thing* for your problems.

Stop looking for excuses why things are not working. Boldly take a stand and allow God's Spirit to guide you.

Whether or not it makes sense to you is not the question. Is it God's Plan? Does it work?

3. They accepted the challenge, overcame the inevitable, and dared to dream the impossible.

As lepers, they were not supposed to have a bright future. Because of their vile condition, they were not expected to achieve anything worthwhile. Yet, God stirred their hearts and they began to believe they *could!* It not only altered their circumstances, but made a difference in the lives of many others. That is what vision does. It allows you to look ahead and prepare yourself for growth.

ATTAIN THE UNATTAINABLE

The lepers did not wait for an invitation to enter the city. Once they positioned themselves *mentally,* they were able to *physically* move into what God had ordained for them. Though they did not have all the facts of what might or might not happen, they had a burning desire to go.

They were in total agreement and did not want to die – nor did they wish to be remembered as pitiful lepers who perished outside the city gate.

These men *did* something to change their future. They redirected their focus. It also drastically changed the destiny of others. Samaria was delivered without even participating in Syria's defeat. Four men, allowing their vision to soar, secured for Samaria what she could not secure for herself.

From this remarkable story, we understand that by changing yourself, you not only affect your circumstance, but you also impact the situation of those around you.

What must change first? *You!*

The pursuit of destiny in God demands a change of identity in us.

MOVE FORWARD

In the Book of Genesis, God asked Abraham to depart from his land, come away from his people, and move to a new place.

Trusting only in what the Lord had told him, Abraham obeyed. Almost as soon as he arrived at the new location, a severe famine swept across the land. He and his family were starving.

In the natural, the move must have seemed ridiculous. But he knew God had spoken, and chose to trust the Lord and participate in His miracle. The Word records, *"Now the Lord had said unto Abram, Get thee out of thy country, and from thy kindred, and from thy father's house, unto a land that I will shew thee: And I will make of thee a great nation, and I will bless thee, and make thy name great; and thou shalt be a blessing: And I will bless them that bless thee, and curse him that curseth thee: and in thee shall all families of the earth be blessed"* (Genesis 12: 1-3).

Although God had asked him to give up everything familiar and comfortable to his life, the Lord replaced those things with immeasurable blessings.

Because of Abraham's willingness to be obedient and make a change, God made a binding agreement with him – an "everlasting covenant" – that could only be broken by apostasy and unfaithfulness.

We too have been extended the same blessings through the Abrahamic covenant and our covenant with Jesus Christ. It was not only for Abraham's immediate family, but also to the future generations who have chosen Jesus as their Lord and Savior. *"Know ye therefore that they which are of faith, the same are the children of Abraham. And the scripture, foreseeing that God would justify the heathen through faith, preached before the gospel unto Abraham, saying, In thee shall all nations be blessed. So then they which be of faith are blessed with faithful Abraham"* (Galatians 3: 7-9).

I will have more to say concerning covenants in Chapter Seven.

THE BLESSING

The word *bless* means "to make holy by religious rite, sanctify, to invoke divine favor upon, to confer wellbeing or prosperity on, to endow as with talent (success)."

In the Hebrew culture, blessings were as treasured as silver and gold. The story of Jacob and Easu (Genesis 25-27) is an excellent example.

Jacob went to great lengths to steal from his brother Esau the firstborn's blessing. They were the twin sons of Isaac and Rebekah.

One day Esau came home from hunting and was tired and hungry. Jacob was cooking a pot of soup and could hardly wait to eat. He said, "Please, Jacob, give me some soup!"

Jacob agreed under one condition – that his older brother would sell him his birthright. (It was a tradition that the birthright belonged to the oldest son, who would receive twice as much inheritance as the other sons, plus the spiritual leadership of the family). Since Esau placed little value on his birthright, he foolishly sold it to Jacob for the meal.

Later, when Isaac became old and his eyesight was deteriorating, it was time for him to transmit his blessing to his favorite son, Esau. He said, *"Now then, get your weapons*

– your quiver and bow – and go out to the open country to hunt some wild game for me. Prepare me the kind of tasty food I like and bring it to me to eat, so that I may give you my blessing before I die" (Genesis 27:3-4).

Rebekah overheard the conversation. The moment Esau left, she ran to Jacob and said, "Quick! Go out and bring me two young goats. I will make your father's favorite meal from them and you will bring it to him. Your father will think you are Esau and will give *you* the blessing!"

Jacob was worried, and said, "Esau is very hairy, and I am not. If my father touches me, he will know I am attempting to trick him. He will curse me, instead of blessing me."

Rebekah replied, *"My son, let the curse fall on me. Just do what I say"* (Genesis 27:13).

Just before Jacob served the meal, his mother dressed him in Easu's clothes and covered his hands and neck with goatskins.

The deceit worked. Here is the blessing intended for Esau, but received by Jacob. *"So he went to him and kissed him. When Isaac caught the smell of his clothes, he blessed him and said, 'Ah, the smell of my son is like the smell of a field that the Lord has blessed. May God give you of heaven's dew and of earth's richness – an abundance of grain and new wine. May nations serve you and peoples bow down to you. Be lord over your brothers, and may the sons of your mother bow down to you. May those who curse you be cursed and those who bless you be blessed"'* (Genesis 27:27-29 NIV).

Although Jacob used deception, he still received favor from God because of the covenant.

Obviously, Esau didn't comprehend the importance of this

divine favor until he had lost it. Upon looking back at his bad decisions, scripture says he burst out with *"a great and exceeding bitter cry,"* (Genesis 27:34) for his father to bless him too. *Any* blessing is better than *no* blessing.

With the favor pronounced upon Jacob, Esau, would now have to serve his brother all the days of his life. Eventually, however, Esau realized the folly of his choices, and how much he had displeased God and his family. He tried to make amends, yet nothing he did would return his original blessing.

A LEGACY

The Hebrew people understood the importance of this scripture: *"I call heaven and earth to record this day against you, that I have set before you life and death, blessing and cursing: therefore choose life, that both thou and thy seed may live"* (Deuteronomy 30:19).

They always pronounced blessings over their children, leaving them with a legacy yet to be fulfilled. The people knew that if they received a covering from God, life would go well and they would walk in success.

Today, we bless our food to sanctify it. We say, "Bless you," to someone when they sneeze. Sadly, the word is often used flippantly.

Perhaps we need to learn to sincerely pray over every situation – and constantly look for the *good*. As the apostle Paul wrote, *"And we know that all things work together for good to them that love God, to them who are the called according to his purpose"* (Romans 8:28).

This does not mean a problem is a positive thing, rather it signifies the outcome through the Lord can be good – if you focus on Him and embrace the purpose to which you are called. The psalmist declared, *"I had fainted, unless I had believed to see the goodness of the Lord in the land of the living"* (Psalm 27:13).

PRESSING TOWARD HIS PURPOSE

There will always be injustice around us, but our goal is to seek justice through Jesus.

Earlier we discussed how Joseph was sold into slavery by his brothers and later thrown into jail because of lies. He was forgotten by those he had helped. That was an incredible amount of unfairness heaped upon one person.

He could have easily looked at what appeared to be discrimination in his life and chosen to become a bitter, angry man. Yet, he was never deterred by the circumstances. Instead, he stayed on course and consistently searched for the silver lining in every situation – pressing toward his purpose. When the events unfolded, Joseph calmly stated, *"You intended to harm me, but God intended it for good to accomplish what is now being done"* (Genesis 50:20, NIV).

I love the words of Robert Schuller: "Tough times never last, but tough people do."

In the midst of the storm, it is good to remember the age-old adage, "This too shall pass."

Circumstances can distract us from God's will, yet everyone has the ability to redirect their focus. That's what

Peter and John did when they faced great obstacles. *"Now when they saw the boldness of Peter and John, and perceived that they were unlearned and ignorant men, they marvelled; and they took knowledge of them, that they had been with Jesus"* (Acts 4:13).

I can relate to that scripture. It tells me that *everyone* has a chance to grow and change through Christ. Peter and John so identified with their spiritual transformation that people were amazed.

Is this power making a change in your life? The apostle Paul prayed, *"That I may know him, and the power of his resurrection and the fellowship of his sufferings, being made conformable unto his death"* (Philippians 3:10).

What a difference Jesus makes!

A REASON FOR CHANGE

In a sinful state, we instinctively know we are not fulfilling God's will.

Our reason to commit to change begins with the creation story. God formed man in His likeness and gave him dominion and power over every living thing.

With the fall of man this was usurped. Yet, when Jesus was resurrected we again received the right to have divine authority over circumstances.

How did God create the universe? By what He *spoke!* Let me emphasize again that your words have the power to curse or bless. *"Death and life are in the power of the tongue"* (Proverbs 18:21).

Make a decision today to speak life – because whatever

you say concerning a situation, it will become. If you want good health, confirm that is what you will have. If you want an outpouring of blessing, speak a scripture of God's abundance. For example, *"Now unto him that is able to do exceeding abundantly above all that we ask or think, according to the power that worketh in us"* (Ephesians 3:20).

Do the same with any area of your life that needs to be strengthened.

MEMORIZE THE WORD

If you want to experience a personal transformation, commit these life-changing scriptures to memory. Speak them out loud and allow the words to resonate through your being:

New wine

"Neither do men put new wine into old bottles: else the bottles break, and the wine runneth out, and the bottles perish: but they put new wine into new bottles, and both are preserved" (Matthew 9:17).

God's correction

"For whom the Lord loveth he correcteth; even as a father the son in whom he delighteth" (Proverbs 3:12).

A completed work

"Being confident of this very thing, that he which hath begun a good work in you will perform it until the day of Jesus Christ" (Philippians 1:6).

Forget the past

"Remember ye not the former things, neither consider the things of old" (Isaiah 43:18).

Something new

"Behold, I will do a new thing; now it shall spring forth; shall ye not know it? I will even make a way in the wilderness, and rivers in the desert" (Isaiah 43:19).

We will be changed

"But we all, with open face beholding as in a glass the glory of the Lord, are changed into the same image from glory to glory, even as by the Spirit of the Lord" (2 Corinthians 3:18).

THE POWER OF DESIRE

The Lord will never force on you what you do not desire. If your heart is not seeking all God has, what can you expect? Nothing! Jesus says *"...ask, and you shall receive"* (John 16:24).

When you have a craving for something, you will figure out a way to obtain it. That's why desire is the eternal force that initiates change.

It is imperative for your future and the advancement of the Kingdom of God to always pursue growth. Without a passion to be transformed, we would never have taken the first step to become a new creation in Christ. At that moment we were *"changed into the same image from glory to glory, even as by the Spirit of the Lord"* (2 Corinthians 3:18). This decision altered our future and revealed a glimpse of our final home – heaven.

As you discover God's plan for your life, let it become your heart's desire. Don't just give mental assent and hope things turn out for the best. Let the vision totally consume you!

With a proper understanding of Spirit-birthed prayer and the willingness to change, you can begin to write your vision and make it plain. Yesterday's problems will not keep you from today's victories. And today's victories will not cause you to become complacent and miss tomorrow's challenges.

Remember this:

- *Change* – allows us to grow.
- *Direction* – causes us to do something we have never done, in order to receive something we have never had, and to go places we have never been.
- *Strength* – allows us to forget our defeats and concentrate on the victories ahead.
- *Hope* – the lifeblood of the vision.
- *Life* – keeps the vision from aborting.

Welcome Change!
Embrace Change!
Celebrate Change!

CHAPTER 5

WRITE THE VISION

*I*f you have ever viewed a piece of art, you understand that it often holds meaning and symbolism far greater than our natural eyes can see. Outstanding literature of any kind – especially poetry and drama – parallels the events of life.

The Bible is the greatest literary treasure known to man and contains incredible examples of God's power. It is a *real* book, with *real* stories and principles that apply to everyday life.

Most important, God's Word is a *written* revelation that speaks to us today. Just as the Lord inspired men and women of old to faithfully record what He said, God is asking us to write the vision He personally gives to you and me.

THE WRITTEN TRUTH

Take your Bible from the shelf and dust it off! Within the pages of God's Word you will find the concepts that reveal the Father's vision, wisdom and knowledge. It is the key to a productive lifestyle.

I am in awe when I read the written accounts of the early patriarchs – how they subdued, conquered and overcame what seemed to be impossible odds. Their understanding of God's

Word combined with their great faith made them more than conquerors.

When I begin to talk about the Bible in terms of blessings, success and prosperity, some brows begin to wrinkle.

Stand on God's Word. Do not be mislead by erroneous beliefs of man, but press on toward the truth.

A CLEAR UNDERSTANDING

Read John Avanzini's book, *Rich God, Poor God.* The scriptural teaching found in this volume will help you be delivered from any spirit of poverty, personal mindset or strongholds that may be holding you back. Dr. Avanzini states there has been an erroneous belief since pre-Reformation days that man's riches are delayed to the hereafter. This mistaken idea has been preached for generations.

The first book of the Bible, Genesis, includes at least six of the most prosperous men found in the Bible – including Abraham. *"...Abram was very rich in cattle, in silver, and in gold"* (Genesis 13:2).

It is also written that *"Poverty and shame shall be to him that refuseth instruction..."* (Proverbs 13:18).

Please understand, I am in no way advocating the principle of *gnosticism* which was similar to a heresy practiced in the Colossian church, and exposed by the apostle Paul.

We cannot be saved through knowledge, only through Jesus Christ. It is important to note, however, to derive the benefits of the Bible, we must apply the hermeneutic principles of interpretation to scripture, as well as the enlightenment given through the Holy Spirit. This better enables us to understand the symbolism used in the Bible. Jesus spoke in parables so that His children could clearly understand the benefits of being overcomers in Christ.

HEED THE WARNING!

Pay close attention to these words: *"Where there is no vision, (no redemptive revelations of God), the people perish: but he that keepeth the law (of God, which includes that of man) blessed, happy, fortunate (and enviable) is he"* (Proverbs 29:18, AMP).

I didn't say this, the Lord did.

Let me tell you what happens when people fail to seek the mind of God. Eli, who was once a priest in Israel, had two worthless sons, Hophni and Phinehas. They had strayed from their official religious duties and had little regard for the things of the Lord. The people told Eli about his sons' many transgressions against the Lord, however, he did not heed their warnings.

Soon, a man of God came to Eli and accused him of honoring his sons more than the Lord. God was angry with Eli and the Scripture says, *"...In those days the word of the Lord was rare; there were not many visions"* (1 Samuel 3:1 NIV).

The man also told Eli that because of his two sons' misdeeds they would die on the same day – and that God would raise up a faithful priest who would obey Him. Eli once again ignored the warnings and did nothing about the situation. Consequently, both of his sons were killed on the same day, when the Philistines attacked Israel and stole the Ark.

What was the Lord's response? He raised up His own man, Samuel, who judged the children of Israel and turned them back to God. Throughout Samuel's lifetime, the Lord continued to give Israel victory against the Philistines.

Because he failed to obey God, Eli lost the blessing the Father had prepared for him.

A GREAT REVELATION

What a contrast we find written in the New Testament. Peter and Cornelius were obedient to what the Lord revealed – and the Gentiles received the blessings of Christianity. In Acts 10 we learn that before Peter had his great vision, he could not comprehend how a Gentile could receive Jesus.

Peter's strict Jewish upbringing led him to believe that Gentiles were inferior people. That became his mindset. It took a revelation from heaven for Peter and Cornelius to realize that *"God is no respecter of persons"* (Acts 10:34). Immediately, they began to fulfil the Lord's desired will.

WRITE IT!

One of the great visionary prophets in Bible times was Habakkuk – his name means "to embrace."

This prophet lived during the reign of Jehoakim, a wicked king who had wandered from God's ways. Judah was in a period of moral and spiritual decay.

Habakkuk, who had a burning zeal for the Lord, cried out for divine intervention. He was very persistent in his appeals to God. *"I will stand upon my watch, and set upon the tower, and will watch to see what he will say to me; and what I shall answer when I am reproved"* (Habakkuk 1: 1).

The Lord's reply came in the form of an unmistakable vision. God instructed the prophet to, *"Write the vision and make it plain upon the tables, that he may run that readeth it. For the vision is yet for an appointed time, but at the end it shall speak and not lie"* (Habakkuk 2:2-3).

It was a true perspective and a divine promise regarding

the outcome of history. Habakkuk had questioned God concerning issues he did not understand, yet the Lord clearly told the prophet to persevere and trust in His covenant promises. They would surely come to pass. God's claims would be universally acknowledged by the whole world.

This took place to ensure that the people did not become weary in the trials they were walking through. God instructed Habakkuk to write what He had revealed – to guarantee *the people would not lose sight of what God was doing and why He was doing it.* The prophet understood and obeyed.

HIS VISION, NOT YOURS

Please don't think that because you sit down and write your vision on a piece of paper it will automatically be fulfilled. If it were that simple, every person on earth would have an incredible life story.

Before you begin to write, you must hear from the Lord through Spirit-birthed prayer.

It must be His vision, not your goals and desires.

Here is a significant scripture: *"And the Lord said unto Abram, after that Lot was separated from him, Lift up now thine eyes, and look from the place where thou art northward, and southward, and eastward, and westward: For all the land which thou seest, to thee will I give it, and to thy seed for ever"* (Genesis 13:14-15).

What is the key? Read the first four words: *"And the Lord said."* It's not our thoughts, but His. It was a heavenly insight that allowed Abraham to increase his earthly sight. He was able to look far across the land.

With God's help, the horizon is limitless! Jesus declared, *"...all things are possible to him that believeth"* (Mark 9:23). That means *you!*

Do not limit your future because of a self-produced prophecy.

When you catch just a glimpse of God's view, everything changes. As Jesus said, *"Your father Abraham rejoiced to see my day: and he saw it, and was glad"* (John 8:56).

DREAM THE IMPOSSIBLE

Franklin Delano Roosevelt, the 32nd President of the United States, led a fascinating life.

Twenty years before his election to the nation's highest office, Roosevelt was already making plans. He and a friend, Louis Howe, energetically created a blueprint for a future campaign. Howe even stepped out in faith and began to call him "Mr. President."

It was a page taken from God's Word. *"While we look not at the things which are seen, but at the things which are not seen"* (2 Corinthians 4:18). The Lord *"...calleth those things which be not as though they were"* (Romans 4:17).

Later, when Roosevelt contracted polio and was bound to a wheelchair, the obstacle did not deter his plan. Certainly there must have been days when he wanted to forget the entire idea, yet his goal created a desire that was greater than any handicap.

Roosevelt continued to move toward his vision and was eventually elected President.

It doesn't matter about your background or the setbacks you have experienced. Pull back the curtain and see clearly His divine purpose for your life. *That's* what you must write!

THE EVIDENCE

The Bible declares, *"Now faith is the substance of things hoped for, the evidence of things not seen"* (Hebrews 11:1).

What is substance? It is a mass that occupies space – usually solid and practical in character. When we speak or write a concept it suddenly takes on substance.

What is the writer of Hebrews telling us? By faith we are to keep God's vision before us. Although it may not yet be manifested in the natural, we have created a *spoken or written plan* whereby we can move toward our desires and goals.

This principle applies to virtually every situation in life – just as the thought of our heavenly home helps us to endure the adversities we face as Christians.

Millions of business people use day-timers and weekly planners to prepare their schedule – often down to the minute. It helps to focus their attention on what needs to be done, and in what order.

We praise the experts who instruct us to make lists for everything in life, not realizing it is the same directive God gave Habakkuk – *"Write the vision and make it plain."*

Have you ever made a grocery list or itemized your "things to do"? I'm sure the answer is "Yes." Many people even keep a journal that records their most intimate details.

Why should it be strange to make a list of the things you want to accomplish for God, yourself, your family or your church? You are simply making it plain – placing something tangible before you, so that you will not lose sight of what the Lord is doing, and why!

SEVEN STEPS

As you prepare to write what God is impressing on your

heart, follow these steps:

1. Find a quiet place to seek God's guidance.

Get alone and spend time in prayer. Begin to have fellowship with your Heavenly Father and ask Him for guidance and direction. Keep your Bible open and make certain the vision lines up with the Word.

Don't make the mistake of choosing a particular scripture that supports what you already want to happen. Read the Word line by line, precept upon precept until you have the assurance this is exactly what God wants you to know.

2. Start writing your vision.

An effective way to get your "writing" juices flowing is to ask yourself questions. "What are the desires God has placed within me? "What are His dreams for my life?"

Then start jotting down what you feel may be the answers. This will help produce clarity and focus concerning God's vision for you.

Don't worry about how the answers may seem to others – and do not try to make this a "perfect" essay that is going to be graded by a professor. Just write as you understand it today. It's the first draft!

3. Fine-tune your list.

After a few days, return to what you placed on paper and do some editing. Be more specific concerning how you see your life being played out.

Start with your long-term vision, which identifies purpose – why we do the things we do. This is what creates value. Ask yourself, "Is it really worth the investment of my time and effort? In the next chapter we will go into detail regarding *counting the cost.*

Help clarify your long-term vision by asking yourself these questions:

- Why do I feel I have this desire?
- How does it fit into my past or present?
- Has my mission changed?
- When my vision is completed, what do I expect to have accomplished?
- Who will it affect?
- How can God be glorified?"

Keep repeating the words of Paul, *"I can do all things through Christ which strengtheneth me"* (Philippians 4:13).

4. Break your long-term vision into short term goals.

Reduce the big objective to a series of small, achievable goals – with each leading you closer to the final destination.

You need a *vehicle* that moves you forward. For example, a farmer's vehicle is his seed; a singer's is a song; a speaker is his message.

Short-term vision helps create the method by which God's long-term dream will be fulfilled.

5. Name the circle of people who influence your life.

On your list, write the names of individuals you believe can help you achieve what the Lord has planned.

- How does your family (spouse, children, relatives) fit in your vision?
- Who are the friends and acquaintances who will play a vital role?

■ What about those in your church or at your work-
place? What is their part?

Remember, *"no man is an island to himself."* Name
those who impact your decisions.

6. Identify your spiritual gifts.
Begin to reflect on the abilities and spiritual gifts God has
placed within you. You may be pleasantly surprised at your
dormant talents.

I recommend that you read the book, *Discover your
Spiritual Gifts,* by Don and Katie Fortune. It will help you
better understand what the Father has given you – as well as
your natural talents.

Scripture tells us, *"For to one is given by the Spirit the
word of wisdom; to another the word of knowledge by the
same Spirit; To another faith by the same Spirit; to another
the gifts of healing by the same Spirit; To another the working
of miracles; to another prophecy; to another discerning of
spirits; to another divers kinds of tongues; to another the
interpretation of tongues: But all these worketh that one and
the selfsame Spirit, dividing to every man severally as he
will"* (1 Corinthians 12:8-11).

We also know that *"Having then gifts differing according
to the grace that is given to us, whether prophecy, let us
prophesy according to the proportion of faith; Or ministry, let
us wait on our ministering: or he that teacheth, on teaching;
Or he that exhorteth, on exhortation: he that giveth, let him
do it with simplicity; he that ruleth, with diligence; he that
sheweth mercy, with cheerfulness"* (Romans 12: 6-8).

Pray and ask the Lord to reveal to you your talents and
abilities. They will lead you on a sure path. *"The steps of a
good man are ordered by the Lord"* (Psalms 37:23).

7. Seek Godly counsel.

Look again at your circle of friends. Which one would you turn to for wisdom and advice. Who has the Lord placed in your path to give you Godly counsel?

The Word says, *"...Believe in the Lord your God, so shall ye be established; believe his prophets, so shall ye prosper"* (2 Chronicles 20:20). We are also told, *"Where no counsel is, the people fall: but in the multitude of counselors there is safety"* (Proverbs 11:14).

What is affirmed by men and women of God may be a confirmation of the vision. *"This is the third time I am coming to you. In the mouth of two or three witnesses shall every word be established"* (2 Corinthians 13:1).

Mike Murdock, in his book *The Law of Recognition,* states that "to recognize the man or woman of God placed in our lives can lead to instant miracles, dramatic changes and prevent a thousand tragedies in your life."

CHART YOUR PROGRESS

These written steps give you a tangible record of where you have started. You will also be able to map your progress.

The psalmist wrote, *"Teach me thy way, O Lord, and lead me in a plain path, because of mine enemies"* (Psalm 27:11). And King Solomon said, *"Commit thy works unto the Lord, and thy thoughts shall be established"* (Proverbs 16:3).

By asking God to be the source of everything in your life, you are calling on Him to be your covenant partner. As in any legal agreement you must ask, "What are my obligations?"

Are you willing to add faith and prayer, to stand on His promises and be faithfully committed to Christ? If so, you are in an excellent position to see God's vision made manifest. *"If ye abide in me, and my words abide in you, ye shall ask what ye will, and it shall be done unto you"* (John 15:7).

WE MADE IT PLAIN

I remember the time our church wished to purchase ten adjacent acres of property for a sanctuary. The price of the land was $1.7 million – much more than was in the current church budget.

Immediately, we heard from the soothsayers who said, "It can never be done," yet we pressed ahead with God's dream.

Rather than attempt to raise the money all at once, we placed banners on each side of the church walls that was a visual, running tally toward our goal. This kept the vision prominently before the congregation – and made it plain for all to see each time they entered the sanctuary.

As we drew closer to our designated goal, excitement intensified. I recall what happened at a New Year's Eve service when we were still short of the necessary funds. That night, as we prayed and looked at the banners, people began to literally rush to the altar with financial gifts – small donations, medium size contributions, and exceedingly large gifts. Praise God, the total amount was raised!

Amazingly, all this transpired in only fourteen months. It was a *written vision* that produced the manifestation of what was needed.

SMALL BEGINNINGS

You may ask, "Where do I start?"

Begin right where you are. The moment God impresses you with a dream – regardless of how trivial it may seem – that's the time to take action.

If you see a need, fill it!

It may seem insignificant, but remember, the servant was told, *"...thou hast been faithful over a few things, I will make thee ruler over many things"* (Matthew 25:23). The Bible also tells us, *"Despise not small beginnings"* (Zechariah 4:10).

If you truly want to find God's vision for your destiny and purpose, be faithful where you are.

"FIX IT!"

During my younger days, when I assisted my father with his church, I was desperately trying to find my place in this world – knowing in my heart of hearts that I was destined to become a pastor some day. However, it wasn't yet time.

One night my father, Bishop Woody, called and said, "Son, I want you to go and fix the toilet at the church." That is exactly what I did. I now realize on that particular evening my purpose in the Kingdom of God was to repair a broken toilet!

What made the life of Jesus so powerful was the fact He was a servant. He served His Father. At the same time He was constantly meeting the needs of others. It was His faithfulness and obedience that ultimately completed God's plan.

Our mission is to minister to those the Lord has placed in our path. As we fulfill His purpose, we become *one* with the heart of God.

THE RIGHT TIME

Live the vision you have written – take ownership of it.

Let me focus again on Habakkuk. Just as God instructed the prophet concerning what was happening in his life, so God will direct you. Oh, you may be tempted to complain, but follow His direction. It's amazing what the Lord will do!

Your vision must become a lifestyle – not a one time event.

When God speaks, don't be surprised if He rebukes you prior to encouraging you.

Before the Lord could reveal to Habakkuk the true meaning of what was happening to him, He had to purify the prophet – to cause him to see things God's way.

The revelation could not occur before Habakkuk surrendered to the fact that God knew best. The outcome did not depend on what was taking place at the moment. The Lord already knew the outcome.

God told the prophet, *"For the revelation awaits an appointed time; it speaks of the end and will not prove false. Though it linger, wait for it; it will certainly come and will not delay"* (Habakkuk 2:3).

It was just a matter of timing – something many believers are not good at understanding. Scripture tells us there is, *"A time to weep, and a time to laugh; a time to mourn, and a time to dance"* (Ecclesiastes 3:4).

DON'T RUSH

Have you ever looked back on a situation and exclaimed, "Wow! It's a good thing I didn't do that!"?

Only when you have become emotionally and mentally prepared to receive what God has for you, will His purpose be fulfilled in your life.

Divine timing is crucial. Your haste may cause the outcome to be premature – which can lead to an aborted plan.

Stop and realize that your present circumstances may not be conducive to receiving your promise. God knows when, where and how. His timing is perfect!

There is a "due season" for everything the Lord does.

Remember what happened when Abraham and Sarah attempted to set their own agenda. (Genesis 2). Oh, the hardship they had to endure.

However, there is more to the story. *God asked, "Is anything too hard for the Lord? I will return to you at the appointed time next year and Sarah will have a son"* (Genesis 18:14 NIV).

It happened! *"Sarah became pregnant and bore a son to Abraham in his old age, at the very time* [season] *God had promised him"* (Genesis 21:2 NIV).

Rest in this assurance: God has your future planned – and He is always on schedule! *"...let us not be weary in well doing: for in due season we shall reap, if we faint not"* (Galatians 6:9).

HE HASN'T CHANGED HIS MIND

I rejoice every time I read the story of Lazarus. He was extremely ill and the doctors could do nothing for him. His sisters, Mary and Martha, called for the Lord to come and heal their brother, but Jesus did not respond immediately, as they had wanted. He waited four days before going to their home, and by that time Lazarus was dead.

They didn't know that when Jesus first learned of Lazarus's condition He made this statement: *"This sickness will not end in death"* (John 11:4 NIV).

Jesus did not say Lazarus would not die, rather that the

story would not conclude that way.

If the Lord had reached the home of Lazarus before he died, the miracle would not have been nearly as effective. The Lord knew the man's sickness would not be unto death. In His spiritual eye He had a revelation of a *living* Lazarus.

He would be raised so that *"God's Son may be glorified through it"* (v.4).

Consider this story with regard to your own life. Perhaps things haven't turned out the way you expected. It may even seem that your dreams have withered or perished.

Don't give up! Jesus will do exactly what He said. He has not forgotten you or changed His mind. What the Lord has planned is etched on the Rock of Ages. He still declares, *"It is written!"* (Matthew 4:4).

SCRIPTURES TO REMEMBER

Commit these scriptures to memory:

Seek a vision

"Where there is no vision, the people perish" (Proverbs 29:18).

Write the vision

"Write the vision, and make it plain upon tables, that he may run that readeth it" (Habakkuk 2:2).

Wait for God's timing

"For the vision is yet for an appointed time, but at the end it shall speak, and not lie: though it tarry, wait for it; because it will surely come, it will not tarry" (Habakkuk 2:3).

The Lord will give you what He shows you
> *"For all the land which thou seest, to thee will I give it, and to thy seed for ever"* (Genesis 13:15).

God will bless what you see
> *"Blessed are the eyes which see the things that ye see"* (Luke 10:23).

Write it! Declare it! Live it!

*T*ake the time to put into words your long-term vision regarding:

My God: _____
_____
_____
_____

Myself: _____
_____
_____
_____

My Family: _____
_____
_____
_____

My Church: _____
_____
_____
_____

CHAPTER 6

COUNT THE COST

*D*on't let your dreams become your nightmares!

Plans and strategies that are thought out illogically are a dark shadow of what is to come. Without counting the cost, you can write the vision a million times to no avail.

How can you help transform God's vision into reality? We are about to look at several ways, however, the key word is *methodology*. Guidelines, procedures, techniques and plans are needed to finish what has been started.

THE "UNSINKABLE" SHIP

The great ocean liner *Titanic* was the pride and joy of the British Empire. On her maiden voyage from Southampton, England to New York City, this "unsinkable" ship slammed into an iceberg 400 miles south of Newfoundland.

On that fateful night, April 15, 1912, more than 1,500 souls perished in the frigid seas. What began as an amazing dream turned into a terrible disaster. What went wrong? Obviously, there were human errors, including faulty planning.

Today, our task is to create a vessel that will withstand the hardships of life's voyage – a fool-proof plan that will not lead to another *Titanic*.

It has been said, "If you don't know where you want to go any road will get you there."

In my observation, if you don't have a precise plan, you'll wind up drifting at sea – or worse!

REACHING THE FINISH LINE

Let's begin with the basics: the plan has a price tag attached – it is going to *cost* you something. Without that advance knowledge, you may suddenly wake up to the fact that the project itself is overwhelming you – and destroying your vision.

What are the costs? Commitment, obedience, wisdom, sacrifice, dedication, persistence, and plenty of faith. If you are not prepared to run with these ideas, don't even begin the race.

Every competitor knows that in order to be a champion there is a personal investment. They begin with preparation and proper planning; and so it is with us.

Someone told me, "Pastor, it doesn't matter how you start, as long as you finish correctly." I strongly disagree with that statement. In fact, the opposite is true. Your beginning greatly impacts your conclusion.

We will never fulfill what God sees for us unless we pay attention to every step – beginning with the first.

You don't have to be in the construction business to know that a house is no stronger than the foundation it stands upon. If the "footings" are not laid correctly, the most well-designed house in the world will one day crumble and fall. It's absolutely essential for the beginning to be carefully engineered.

THE TWO FROGS

Author Dutch Sheets shared a poem about two frogs. It is a lesson on what it takes to become a winner.

>*Two frogs fell into a can of cream,*
>   *Or so it has been told.*
>*The sides of the can were shiny and steep,*
>   *The cream was deep and cold.*
>*"Oh, what's the use," said number one,*
>   *It's plain no help's around.*
>*"Good-bye, my friend, good-bye, sad world,"*
>   *And weeping still he drowned.*
>*But number two, of sterner stuff,*
>   *Dog-paddled in surprise.*
>*The while he licked his creamy lips,*
>   *And blinked his creamy eyes.*
>*"I'll swim at least a while," he thought,*
>   *Or so it has been said.*
>*It really wouldn't help the world,*
>   *If one more frog were dead.*
>*An hour or more he kicked and swam,*
>   *Not once he stopped to mutter.*
>*Then hopped out from the island he had*
>   *Made of fresh churned butter.*
>   *– Author unknown*

WHAT'S THE ESTIMATE?

The bottom line of completing God's dream for your life is found in this parable. Jesus said, *"Suppose one of you wants to build a tower. Will he not first sit down and estimate the cost to see if he has enough money to complete it? For if he lays the foundation and is not able to finish it, everyone who sees it will ridicule him, saying, 'This fellow began to build and was not able to finish'"* (Luke 14:28-30 NIV).

Cost counting! That's what your Father expects.

Think about the rich young ruler who ran up to Jesus *"...and fell on his knees before him. 'Good teacher,' he asked, 'what must I do to inherit eternal life?'"* (Mark 10:17 NIV).

"'Why do you call me good?' Jesus answered. 'No one is good – except God alone. You know the commandments: Do not murder, do not commit adultery, do not steal, do not give false testimony, do not defraud, honor your father and mother'" (vv. 19-19).

"'Teacher,' he declared, 'all these I have kept since I was a boy'" (v.20).

Jesus looked at him with love and compassion. *"'One thing you lack,' He said. 'Go, sell everything you have and give to the poor, and you will have treasure in heaven. Then come, follow me'"* (v.21).

The Bible records, *"At this the man's face fell. He went away sad, because he had great wealth"* (Mark 10:22).

The young man counted the cost and decided it was too steep. The price was more than he was willing to pay – yet think of the blessing he missed!

THE PRICE!

You will never have a victory without a battle!

Read the stories of Abraham, Moses, David, and Joseph. They all endured great trials in order to receive the promises of God. Scripture also details the sad fate of those who were not willing to pay the price of commitment and obedience.

They lost everything God had prepared for them.

It is the determined, and those willing to sacrifice – the ones who never give up! The Bible says, *"And from the days of John the Baptist until now the kingdom of heaven suffereth violence, and the violent take it by force."* (Matthew 11:12).

STARTING FROM SCRATCH

I know from experience what it is like to be around someone who never gave up. My father is such as man.

Bishop Woody Thomas was called into ministry when he was seventeen years old and served in the denominational ranks for the next forty years. At the age of fifty-nine he was emotionally tired, physically sick and financially broke.

Fervently, he sought heaven for answers – and one day captured the mind of God. The Lord began to reveal to him, "I want you to start a church in Margate, Florida!"

He obeyed God's command and started from scratch – with eleven people, $14 and a little poodle dog! Armed with those meager resources and the Lord's divine direction, he birthed the church I now pastor. That's why I say, "Thanks Dad, for being a man of commitment, obedience and vision!"

ONLY THE BEGINNING!

The cost of accomplishing something worthwhile almost always involves blood, sweat and tears. It is nothing new. That is what Jesus endured in the Garden of Gethsemane.

When the Lord faced the most critical moment of decision in His life, He said, *"Now is my soul troubled; and what shall I say? Father, save me from this hour: but for this cause came I unto this hour. Father, glorify thy name. Then came there a voice from heaven, saying, I have both glorified it, and will glorify it again"*(John 12:27-28).

Christ knew the price He was about to pay – for Himself and others. That is why Jesus did not run from His Father's will. When He declared, *"It is finished"* (John 19:30), that was only the beginning. Three days later He gained *resurrection power!*

The victory of Christ came at the price of obedience, commitment and sacrifice. That's what He is asking of you and me.

DREAM ON!

As a young child, Matthew Barnett, asked his father,

> *"Dad, do you think it's possible to build a church that would be open twenty-four hours a day?"*

He repeated the question again and again, and his father, Tommy Barnett, pastor of a great congregation in Phoenix, Arizona, would always give the same reply, "Son, I've never heard about a church like that, but why don't you become the first person to do it?"

Matthew believed that if you have just one idea, one dream, and you never let it die, there would be a day when everything would somehow come together. And come together it did!

In his book, *The Church that Never Sleeps*, Matthew Barnett shares how, at the age of twenty, he began working with the homeless, those on welfare, and the street people. From there he went on to buy a $4 million building in downtown Los Angeles and created what is known as the "Dream Center"– truly the church that never sleeps!

It has over 200 ministries in the community, including abandoned children, the hungry, the homeless and those addicted to alcohol and drugs. It is a refuge for every person whose hope has been shattered and needs to dream again.

Matthew accomplished exactly what God had placed in his mind as a child.

THE ULTIMATE PRICE

Dr. Martin Luther King, too, had a dream. He saw a day when blacks were no longer sitting in the back of the bus!

Ridiculed and scorned, the leader of the Civil Rights Movement forged ahead with the vision God had given him. He became one of the most prominent figures of his time.

King not only counted the cost, but on a fateful day in Memphis, Tennessee, paid the ultimate price for the commitment to his cause. His dream, however, did not die. It lives on, growing with each passing day.

ACCEPT THE CHALLENGE

Before taking action, every successful CEO and corporate leader makes a plan and determines the cost. That's what Lee Iacocca did when he took the helm of the faltering Chrysler Corporation. Sales were sinking and the company desperately needed a major overhaul.

It was an emergency! Drastic changes had to be made in order to keep the company afloat. It was a huge task that would require laser-like personal attention and mass reorganization. Iacocca knew the toll it would exact – both on the corporation and on his personal life.

He not only accepted the challenge, he led one of the greatest corporate comebacks in history.

THE RESULTS

Dreams are essential – and so is commitment. That's what makes a "never give up" attitude possible. When God shows you the end from the beginning, obstacles begin to shrink. You learn now to climb over, go around, and even tunnel under them. When failure causes you to fall, you simply get back up!

Here are the results of total commitment:

1. Commitment causes us to face our fears.

Since God's vision is going to take us places we have never been and cause us to do things we have never done, it stands to reason that there may be something along the way that will attempt to frighten us. The good news is: "...perfect love casteth out fear" (1 John 4:18).

God's love in you, and your love for Him, combines to rid you of the fear of the unknown. Instead of fretting over what you *can't* do, remind yourself again and again that, *"I can do all things through Christ which strengtheneth me"* (Philippians 4:13).

Like David facing Goliath, you no longer ignore the giant blocking your way. The obstacle is removed by the power of the Almighty and the desire He has placed within you to achieve.

2. Commitment requires us to take personal responsibility.

You can no longer blame anyone else for your failures or your problems, nor can you allow the experiences of yesterday to dictate what you will accomplish today. No more passing the buck!

The past is the past – let it go! Move on and don't be

tempted to look back. As the apostle Paul declared with confidence: *"...for I know whom I have believed, and am persuaded that he is able to keep that which I have committed unto him against that day"* (2 Timothy 1:12). This *knowing* makes our future bright.

3. Commitment causes us to accept the challenges of life.

Every day there are opportunities for the glory of God to be revealed and released. Life may not always be fair, yet God is good.

What about the Evil One who comes against us? *"The Lord shall laugh at him: for he seeth that his day is coming. The wicked have drawn out the sword, and have bent their bow, to cast down the poor and needy, and to slay such as be of upright conversation"* (Psalm 37:13-14).

Stay committed!

GOOD ENOUGH!

God tells us to trust – and also to obey.

Abraham understood this completely. The "father of nations" listened to the Lord and left his homeland, not knowing where he was headed.

Much later, *"...after he had patiently endured, he obtained the promise"* (Hebrews 6:15).

God said he would receive an inheritance – and that was good enough for Abraham.

Even when he was asked to offer up his son, Isaac, as a living sacrifice, he responded without question. Obedience was Abraham's lifestyle, and it resulted in great blessing.

OBEYING THE FATHER

Jesus told the story of a man who had two sons. He went to the first and said, *"Son, go and work today in the vineyard"* (Matthew 21:28 NIV).

The son refused, but later changed his mind and went. *"Then the father went to the other son and said the same thing. He answered, 'I will, sir,' but he did not go'"* (v.30).

"'Which of the two did what his father wanted?' "The first," they answered. Jesus said to them, 'I tell you the truth, the tax collectors and the prostitutes are entering the kingdom of God ahead of you. For John came to you to show you the way of righteousness, and you did not believe him, but the tax collectors and the prostitutes did. And even after you saw this, you did not repent and believe him'" (vv.31-32).

If you are looking for a prayer of obedience, speak the words of the psalmist: *"Teach me, O Lord, the way of thy statutes; and I shall keep it unto the end. Give me understanding, and I shall keep thy law; yea, I shall observe it with my whole heart. Make me to go in the path of thy commandments; for therein do I delight"* (Psalm 119:33-35).

A HIGH PRICE

Refusal to obey leads to the sin of rebellion.

From early in His ministry, Jesus knew who would deny or betray Him. After teaching in the synagogue at Capernaum, *"From that time many of his disciples went back, and walked no more with him. Then said Jesus unto the twelve, Will ye also go away?"* (John 6:66-67).

Think of it! They knew the Lord, yet turned away – not willing to pay the price for obedience and commitment.

We must never forget that scripture states: *"Behold, to obey is better than sacrifice...For rebellion is as the sin of witchcraft"* (1 Samuel 15:22-23 KJV).

Disobedience carries a high price tag. Be thankful you serve a God of second chances.

Jesus makes it clear that only through submission and faithfulness do we have the right to call on His name. He asked, *"Why do you call me, 'Lord, Lord,' and do not do what I say? I will show you what he is like who comes to me and hears my words and puts them into practice. He is like a man building a house, who dug down deep and laid the foundation on rock. When a flood came, the torrent struck that house but could not shake it, because it was well built. But the one who hears my words and does not put them into practice is like a man who built a house on the ground without a foundation. The moment the torrent struck that house, it collapsed and its destruction was complete"* (Luke 6:46-49 NIV).

THE BODY

Start practicing commitment and obedience in just *one* area of your life and watch what happens. For example, obey God's call to regularly attend church. Many people cannot seem to do it without grumbling or complaining.

Why should the Father ask you to do something of great value if you are not willing to follow Him in what is basic?

Scripture says, *"Not forsaking the assembling of ourselves together..."* (Hebrews 10:25). That means, *go to church!*

115

The reason we need to discipline ourselves to attend the house of God regularly is because the Lord, Himself, has joined us to the local assembly of believers. Remember, *"...ye are the body of Christ, and members in particular"* (1 Corinthians.12:27). *"But now hath God set the members every one of them in the body, as it hath pleased him"* (1 Corinthians. 12:18). *"From whom the whole body fitly joined together and compacted by that which every joint supplieth, according to the effectual working in the measure of every part, maketh increase of the body unto the edifying of itself in love"* (Ephesians 4:16).

It is within the corporate structure of the house of God that we discover *who* we are and *why* we are here. The church is also where the Lord teaches us the secret of serving others.

We are not called to be detached from each other, rather mutually interdependent. Only a servant rises to the level of a master – and only a follower can become a leader.

If our desire to serve is obstructed, then our vision for success will be obscured. Jesus was both a King and a servant.

> *On the wall of a football locker room, the coach wrote these words: Nobody Wins Until We All Win.*

How true. United we stand, divided we fall!

The Lord desires that we are one in mind, body, soul and spirit. Jesus said, *"That they all may be one; as thou, Father, art in me, and I in thee, that they also may be one in us, that the world may believe that thou hast sent me"* (John 17:21).

THE LOVE FACTOR

If you want to know the mind of God, begin to understand that His ultimate investment in you is summed up in one word: *love*. It is the reason He sent His Son to earth, and the measuring stick by which He expects us to live.

Before Christ ascended to heaven, He said, *"A new commandment I give unto you, That ye love one another; as I have loved you, that ye also love one another. By this shall all men know that ye are my disciples, if ye have love one to another"* (John 13:34-35 NIV)

How do we know we have passed from death unto life? *"...because we love our brothers. Anyone who does not love remains in death. Anyone who hates his brother is a murderer, and you know that no murderer has eternal life in him"* (1 John 3:14-15).

The Word declares, *"If anyone says, 'I love God,' yet hates his brother, he is a liar. For anyone who does not love his brother, whom he has seen, cannot love God, whom he has not seen. And he has given us this command: Whoever loves God must also love his brother"* (1 John 4:20-21 NIV).

YOUR SOURCE OF WISDOM

Just as the Father bestows love on His children, He also imparts *wisdom*. The thinking of most men is human rather than heavenly. Only when we seek the thoughts of the Creator do we find true knowledge.

Scripture declares, *"Through wisdom is an house builded; and by understanding it is established: And by knowledge shall the chambers be filled with all precious and pleasant riches"* Proverbs 24:3- 4). King Solomon knew the value of wisdom and desired it more than silver and gold.

How do we receive the mind of God? Simply ask! *"If any*

of you lack wisdom, let him ask of God, that giveth to all men liberally, and upbraideth not; and it shall be given him" (James 1:5).

Why is the wisdom of the Father so important? It allows us to know the difference between wise and foolish choices. *"For the Lord gives wisdom, and from his mouth come knowledge and understanding. He holds victory in store for the upright, he is a shield to those whose walk is blameless, for he guards the course of the just and protects the way of his faithful ones. Then you will understand what is right and just and fair – every good path"* (Proverbs 2:6-9 NIV).

The apostle Paul asked God *"to fill you with the knowledge of his will through all spiritual wisdom and understanding"* (Colossians 1:8).

HE'S GOOD!

Counting the cost of the vision should not be a drudgery. Not at all. I believe Oral Roberts was divinely inspired of the Lord to make these five words a basic principle of his ministry: *God is a good God!*

Look again at the words you have written about your future. Does it line up with the knowledge that He is *good* – that He loves you and wants to bless you?

I feel sorry for those who believe the Lord constantly desires to punish and chastise them. If that were true, what sense does it make for God to deliver you from any problem you are going through.

Certainly the Father is sovereign, but since the fall of man, the law of "sowing and reaping" has been a foundational principle. It is still in effect. God has not dealt you a bad hand in life. Your war is with the devil or yourself, not with the Creator.

No one hurts more than the Heavenly Father when He

watches the perils we encounter because of disobedience and apostasy. Jesus came to give you something beautiful, something grand. Get this in your spirit! *"The thief cometh not, but for to steal, and to kill, and to destroy: I am come that they might have life, and that they might have it more abundantly"* (John 10:10).

DOUBLE-MINDED

Look again at Chapter Three and pay close attention to the words of the Lord's Prayer that says, *"... thy will be done on earth, as it is in heaven"* (Matthew 6:10).

Determine the cost of doing His will, not yours. Otherwise you will become what is described in the Epistle of James. He declares, *"...this person is a double-minded man unstable in all his ways"* (James 1:8).

Unless your thoughts and your actions are united, you will never produce what God intends. Rather, you will become as the descendants of Noah. With great ambition they built the Tower of Babel, yet it collapsed. Don't fall into that trap.

HE NEEDS YOU

On your journey to find God's vision:

- Understand that the Lord *needs* you. There is something that He wants you to do that no one else can accomplish.
- Take responsibility for yourself. Don't blame others for things that aren't working in your life, and don't wait for others to make things happen for you.
- Pray to discern God's *methodology* for fulfilling the vision.

119

- Ask the Lord to assist you with His ideas, concepts and strategies to "walk out" your destiny.
- Realize that you have value and purpose.
- Call on the Holy Spirit – your counselor and guide.

Only by continually reminding yourself of your vision will you be willing to pay the price required to maintain your commitment. It is God's love and wisdom, plus your obedience that will ultimately assure you success.

H. Jackson Brown included these words in *Life's Little Instruction Book*:

You pay a price for getting stronger
You pay a price for getting faster
You pay a price for jumping higher
(But you also), pay a price for staying just the same.

To finish first, you must first finish!

CHAPTER 7

IT'S A PROMISE!

During the 1800s a young man in Europe dreamed about coming to America. He visualized the new frontier and believed in his heart that fortune awaited him on those distant shores.

After saving just enough money, he booked passage on an ocean liner and began his journey of a lifetime.

As the ship arrived in New York, the adventurer was ready to disembark when the captain noticed him and said, "Son, I saw you get on the ship, but I haven't seen you again until now. Where were you during the meal times. I didn't see you at breakfast, lunch or dinner. Where have you been keeping yourself?"

The young man lowered his head and responded, "You don't understand, sir. I only had enough money to pay for the ticket."

The captain was stunned! He said, "Son, didn't you know that in the price of the ticket, your food was included – all paid for?"

What a shame. The boy had been eating moldy cheese and old bread, with just enough water to survive the voyage. If he had only known, he could have been dining at the captain's table.

Sadly, there are many in the body of Christ who are surviving on yesterday's manna. They have a foresight of their destination, and desire to reach it, yet they don't have a revelation of the finished work of the cross. They do not possess what is already theirs!

ALREADY PAID!

Everything we need is within our grasp – if we would only reach out. Jesus talked about people whose hearts have turned cold. *"...their ears are dull of hearing, and their eyes they have closed; lest at any time they should see with their eyes and hear with their ears, and should understand with their heart, and should be converted, and I should heal them"* (Matthew 13:15).

Just like the young man on the ocean liner, as a Christian you have been given rights. They are part of your passage to heaven that was paid for at Calvary.

The blood of Christ has been applied to your heart and you are an heir of the Father. As such, you have certain privileges that are included in your inheritance. It is a binding contract – an agreement and partnership with God.

THE MARKS OF THE LORD

You are *marked!*

This means God is totally committed to helping you achieve what He has planned – even if you make mistakes and stumble along the way.

> *What is in His mind is now in yours. Suddenly, the odds are in your favor.*

The word *mark* was commonly used in the Greek language as a description of a type of branding that identified the ownership of a slave. Paul often referred to himself as a bondservant of the Lord. He was "marked and bound" to Christ. As the apostle wrote to the believers at Galatia, *"From henceforth let no man trouble me: for I bear in my body the marks of the Lord Jesus"* (Galatians 6:17).

It is this mark that entitles you to everything owned by your Father – in heaven and on earth. This knowledge will allow you walk in the abundance God has for your life which is to *"...prosper and be in health, even as thy soul prospereth"* (3 John 2).

Here are just a few who have been marked by God:

Samson

From his very birth, Samson was set apart for greatness. *"A certain man of Zorah, named Manoah, from the clan of the Danites, had a wife who was sterile and remained childless. The angel of the Lord appeared to her and said, 'You are sterile and childless, but you are going to conceive and have a son. Now see to it that you drink no wine or other fermented drink and that you do not eat anything unclean, because you will conceive and give birth to a son. No razor may be used on his head, because the boy is to be a Nazirite, set apart to God from birth, and he will begin the deliverance of Israel from the hands of the Philistines'"* (Judges 13:2-5 NIV).

Samson was chosen for a special purpose.

Daniel

God also marked Daniel.

With quiet submission Daniel was positioned in the palace to fulfill the call upon his life. It wasn't the young man's ego or ambition that placed him there. The Bible says, *"Now God had brought Daniel into favor..."*(Daniel 1:9).

Because of his talent, knowledge, understanding and integrity, Daniel rose to a high rank in the palace of King Nebuchadnezzar. Later, when he was thrown into a den of lions, the Lord delivered him, *"...because he had trusted in his God"* (Daniel 6:23 NIV).

Esther

When Haman was about to exterminate all of the Jewish people during the reign of Mordecai, Esther found favor with the king. She was marked by God, *"for such a time as this"* (Esther 4:14).

At a great banquet, Esther asked this request of the king. She said, *"If I have found favor with you, O king, and if it pleases your majesty, grant me my life – this is my petition. And spare my people – this is my request"* (Esther 7:3).

Not only was her wish granted, but Haman was hanged.

THE COVENANT!

When we understand the concept of *covenants,* we are able to better comprehend the incredible legal rights God has granted to His children.

The word "testament" means covenant. That is what we have in both the Old and New Testament. A covenant spells out the stipulations of an agreement between parties – and usually details the consequences of not fulfilling your part of the bargain. The purpose is so that you may establish a strong partnership.

There are many covenants described in scripture. Let

me suggest that you make a personal study of the subject to see how those of the Old Testament were a foreshadow of the "new and better" era that came with Christ.

Let's look at the four major covenants included in God's Word:

1. The Abrahamic Covenant

The Almighty made an agreement with Abraham that promised, *"I will make you into a great nation and I will bless you; I will make your name great, and you will be a blessing. I will bless those who bless you, and whoever curses you I will curse; and all peoples on earth will be blessed through you"* (Genesis 12:2-3 NIV).

God's pact included more than land – and it was promised to his descendants (Genesis 15:18).

The Lord stipulated that He would provide the blessings of provision, protection, direction and guidance. It was a sovereign promise of God.

Abraham kept his part of the bargain – and the Lord certainly kept His. Four hundred years later, the Bible records that *"...God heard their groaning, and God remembered his covenant with Abraham, with Isaac, and with Jacob"* (Exodus 2:24).

When we read the story of this great man of God, the circumstances often looked grim. In the natural, everything seemed bleak for Abraham and his descendants. Yet, God is bound by His covenants. He always fulfills the promise.

2. The Mosaic Covenant

Through Moses, God made an agreement with the nation of Israel at Mount Sinai (Exodus 19-24).

The Mosaic Covenant separated Israel as people unto

God. He said, *"...you will be for me a kingdom of priests and a holy nation"* (Exodus 19:6 NIV).

The Lord not only spoke to Moses, but the contract was written in stone. He *"was there with the Lord forty days and forty nights; he did neither eat bread, nor drink water. And he wrote upon the tables the words of the covenant, the ten commandments"* (Exodus 34:28).

The blessings promised to the children of Israel were conditional – they must keep God's Law. Failure to uphold the covenant would forfeit their rights.

The Mosiac Law included a sacrificial system as a means of temporal forgiveness – to restore their fellowship with God. These offerings were only a symbol of a coming Messiah that would provide the final sacrifice.

3. The Davidic Covenant

Through a specific pact with David, God continued what He began with Abraham. *"I have made a covenant with my chosen, I have sworn unto David my servant, Thy seed will I establish for ever, and build up thy throne to all generations"* (Psalm 89:3-4).

Under David, Israel possessed almost all the land that had been promised to the Israelites. *"Which covenant he made with Abraham, and his oath unto Isaac; And confirmed the same unto Jacob for a law, and to Israel for an everlasting covenant"* (Psalm 105:9-10).

The Davidic Covenant is described in 2 Samuel 7 and includes this promise from God: *"I will...give you rest from all your enemies. The Lord declares to you that the Lord himself will establish a house for you"* (2 Samuel 7:11).

It was a house that would not be destroyed. God said, *"I will establish your line forever and make your throne firm through all generations"* (Psalms 89:4).

The "House of David" would lead directly to the birth of Christ. As Paul would write centuries later, *"Concerning his Son Jesus Christ our Lord, which was made of the seed of David according to the flesh"* (Romans 1:3).

4. The New Covenant

The prophet Jeremiah spoke of the day when a new testament would replace the old. *"But this shall be the covenant that I will make with the house of Israel; After those days, saith the Lord, I will put my law in their inward parts, and write it in their hearts; and will be their God, and they shall be my people"* (Jeremiah 31:33).

God declared, *"Behold, the days come, saith the Lord, when I will make a new covenant with the house of Israel and with the house of Judah"* (Hebrews 8:8).

What the Father instituted at the cross was *"...a better covenant, which was established upon better promises"* (Hebrews 8:6).

> *Jesus became the sacrificial Lamb that forever atoned for our sin – the mediator between God and man.*

"For by one offering he hath perfected for ever them that are sanctified" (Hebrews 10:14).

"ALL THINGS"

The death, burial and resurrection of Jesus made it possible for you to receive the blessings of Abraham – and more. God has made you an heir, in line for eternal provisions.

Scripture declares, *"But when the fullness of the time was come, God sent forth his Son, made of a woman, made under the law, To redeem them that were under the law, that we might receive the adoption of sons. And because ye are sons, God hath sent forth the Spirit of his Son into your hearts, crying, Abba, Father. Wherefore thou art no more a servant, but a son; and if a son, then an heir of God through Christ"* (Galatians 4:4-7).

That is good news! *"And if ye be Christ's, then are ye Abraham's seed, and heirs according to the promise"* (Galatians 3:29).

How did the Lord bless Abraham? In *"all things"* (Genesis 24:1).

Deuteronomy 28 tells us what is involved in our inheritance. If we harken to the voice of the Lord and obey His commandments, *"...all these blessings shall come on thee, and overtake thee"* (Deuteronomy 28:2).

In the verses that follow we are promised:

Honor
Blessedness
Prosperity
Victory
God's favor
Good health

THE MARK THAT MATTERS

I pray that you truly understand who you are in Christ. You have been marked for an inheritance. Satan recognizes that fact and still targets you to someday receive his mark – *666* (Revelation 13:18).

Perhaps those in our society who wear tattoos instinctively realize that we are to bear a mark. How I wish they would all come to know this truth:

The only mark that matters is the one Christ writes on our hearts.

Your position in the Kingdom is that of *"...an heir of God and a joint heir with Christ"* (Romans 8:17).

The Word tells us that, *"As you come to him, the living Stone – rejected by men but chosen by God and precious to him – you also, like living stones, are being built into a spiritual house to be a holy priesthood, offering spiritual sacrifices acceptable to God through Jesus Christ. For in Scripture it says: 'See, I lay a stone in Zion, a chosen and precious cornerstone, and the one who trusts in him will never be put to shame'"* (1 Peter 2:4-6 NIV).

Rejoice in the fact that *"...you are a chosen people, a royal priesthood, a holy nation, a people belonging to God, that you may declare the praises of him who called you out of darkness into his wonderful light"* (v.9).

It doesn't get any better than this! Because of the substitutionary work completed on the cross by our Lord Jesus Christ, we have inherited the gifts and promises fit for a King.

REDEEMED! REDEEMED!

Understand that you were nailed to that cross with Christ, raised with Him, and now sit at the right hand of the Father with Jesus. He not only became sin for us, but also a *curse* so that we would be in line for all of God's blessings. *"Christ hath redeemed us from the curse of the law, being made a curse for us: for it is written, Cursed is every one that hangeth on a tree: That the blessing of Abraham might come on the Gentiles through Jesus Christ; that we might receive the promise of the Spirit through faith"* (Galatians 3:13-14).

The apostle Paul sternly reprimands the members of the church at Galatia for falling back into the works of the law, rather than living by grace and faith. *"O foolish Galatians, who hath bewitched you, that ye should not obey the truth, before whose eyes Jesus Christ hath been evidently set forth, crucified among you? This only would I learn of you, Received ye the Spirit by the works of the law, or by the hearing of faith"* (Galatians 3:1-2).

They had fallen into *dead works*.

Paul summed up his point. *"What I mean is this: The law, introduced 430 years later, does not set aside the covenant previously established by God and thus do away with the promise. For if the inheritance depends on the law, then it no longer depends on a promise; but God in his grace gave it to Abraham through a promise"* (Galatians 3:17-18 NIV).

YOUR JOURNEY

Rest in God's promises. He will take you:

From your Egypt to your Canaan.
From your bondage to your freedom.
From your sickness to your health.
From your poverty to your prosperity.
From your failure to your success.
From your weakness to your strength.

WHERE IS YOUR TRUST?

Don't make the mistake of placing your faith and trust in men, or in the law. It opens the door for carnality and legalism – and can bring a curse on your life.

Speaking through the prophet Jeremiah, God said, *"Cursed is the one who trusts in man, who depends on flesh for his strength and whose heart turns away from the Lord. He will be like a bush in the wastelands; he will not see prosperity when it comes. He will dwell in the parched places of the desert, in a salt land where no one lives"* (Jeremiah 17:5-6).

If you began something in the spirit and have since fallen into the flesh, the simple solution is confession and repentance. This will return you to restoration and intimate fellowship with Jesus. Bring your life into subjection to God's standard of holiness and you will reap His blessing.

TAKE POSSESSION

You must *choose* to seek the mind of God. Position yourself so that He can lead you each step of the journey.

That's what Joshua did. He was told by the Lord to take possession of the promised land – the inheritance of the children of Israel.

Although God had given them the *right* to the land, they had to fight many battles to obtain what was rightfully theirs. The Lord said, *"Moses my servant is dead; now therefore arise, go over this Jordan, thou, and all this people, unto the land which I do give to them, even to the children of Israel. Every place that the sole of your foot shall tread upon, that have I given unto you, as I said unto Moses"* (Joshua 1:2-3).

God is still in the business of protection, provision and blessings. It is sad to see people miss so many of the gifts the Father has already prepared for them.

It is time to reach out and possess what is yours!

KNOW YOUR RIGHTS!

As children of Abraham we have divine rights! Jesus recognized this when He healed a woman who had a spirit of infirmity for eighteen years (Luke 13:11-13).

The ruler of the synagogue was indignant because Jesus had healed on the Sabbath. To the criticism, the Lord replied, *"And ought not this woman, being a daughter of Abraham, whom Satan hath bound, lo, these eighteen years, be loosed from this bond on the sabbath day?"* (Luke 13:16).

This was a covenant privilege as a daughter of Abraham. She had a right and Jesus knew it! Healing was part of her inheritance as a child of the King!

IN THE DEVIL'S FACE!

I laughed when I heard the story of an atheist who lived next door to a poor, elderly Christian woman. She was a widow. Every day the woman walked out on her front porch, loudly praising God for provisions in her life.

The unbeliever witnessed this scene so many times that he finally became furious and said to himself,

"I can't take this anymore. I'm going to prove to her there is no God."

One morning, he rushed to the store and bought two full bags of groceries. After he sneaked them on her front porch, he hid in the bushes.

When the woman opened the door, she saw the groceries and started shouting and praising God – louder than ever!

Leaping from the bushes, the atheist yelled at her, "You see, there is no God. It was *me* who bought those bags of food!"

She paused for a moment, then continued praising the Lord again. The man was bewildered when she looked up to heaven and said, "God, I praise and thank You for making the devil go out and buy me these groceries!"

The woman knew the source of her provision, and how to possess what God had provided. She also knew how to rub it in the devil's face!

PLANTING GOD'S SEED

Oral Roberts, one of the most prominent expositors of today's faith movement, expanded my vision regarding the concept of seedtime and harvest.

After an ORU Board of Regents meeting in Tulsa, Oklahoma, we were on a flight together. I asked him what I felt to be a deep theological question, one that I was sure would absorb the entire time of the trip.

"Dr. Roberts, where do you think the body of Christ has missed it?"

He leisurely unwrapped his favorite candy bar *(Bit of Honey)*, then casually turned to me and said, *"They leave their harvest in the field."*

I paused for a moment and responded, "Hmm ...interesting! Would you like to expound on that statement?"

"Certainly," he said, "*Study it for yourself!*"

He plumped his pillow and went to sleep, and I did the same. However, I knew I had been given profound wisdom, and later spent a great deal of time delving into the topic.

SEED TIME

Here is what I learned. When a farmer gets ready to plant his seed, he knows that before he can actually begin, he must first prepare the ground. This means a great deal of tilling and plowing.

The soil might even require the removal of stones, sticks and other obstacles. The farmer knows that he can't just haphazardly throw the seed on unprepared ground and expect to reap the bounty of his labors. It takes planning and hard work.

There is a tremendous lesson in the *parable of the sower* (Mark 4). It shows the necessity of walking in the Word, and knowing the mind of God.

Jesus told the story of a man who spread his seed in a variety of places:

- Some fell by the wayside and the fowls of the air came and devoured it (Mark 4:4).
- Some fell on stony ground, and when it came up, withered away (v.6).
- Some fell among thorns. When the seed sprouted, the thorns choked it (v.7).
- Other seeds fell on good ground and brought a great increase (v.8).

Jesus explained that the parable had a far greater meaning. He said, *"The sower soweth the word"* (Mark 4:14).

There were four groups involved:

1. The first group was exposed to the Word, but that didn't ensure a harvest.

Jesus said that some people *"...are like seed along the path, where the word is sown. As soon as they hear it, Satan comes and takes away the word that was sown in them"* (Mark 4:15 NIV).

Many have received seed from God, yet allow the devil to plunder what has been planted.

2. The second received the Word, but didn't take ownership of it.

These people actually let God enter their lives, however, they didn't embrace His will as their own. As the Lord explained, *"Others, like seed sown on rocky places, hear the word and at once receive it with joy. But since they have no root, they last only a short time. When trouble or persecution comes because of the word, they quickly fall away"* (vv.16-17).

Rather than cultivating the hard stony ground, they grew weary in well doing – becoming offended that God had asked for extra effort.

3. The third group took ownership, then perverted it for their own selfish gain.

Jesus said, *"Still others, like seed sown among thorns,*

hear the word; but the worries of this life, the deceitfulness of wealth and the desires for other things come in and choke the word, making it unfruitful" (vv.18-19).

Over the years I have met people who knew the mind of the Father, yet, because of personal ambition, walked out on His plan.

4. The fourth group sowed in good ground and received a bountiful harvest.

"Others, like seed sown on good soil, hear the word, accept it, and produce a crop – thirty, sixty or even a hundred times what was sown" (v.20).

So fertile was their ground that the Word became, *"a lamp unto their feet and a light unto their path"* (Psalm 119:105).

They experienced the reward doing things *His* way.

IT'S NEVER TOO LATE!

Regardless of your age, bank account, education or ancestry, if God plants a seed in your mind and heart, He intends for it to flourish.

Embrace what has been sown and start watering your crop. There is still time for reaping.

Jesus spoke to that issue when He likened the Kingdom of Heaven to *"...a landowner who went out early in the morning to hire men to work in his vineyard"* (Matthew 20:1 NIV). He agreed to pay them a certain wage for the day's labor.

Later in the day, another group of workers came and the master hired them, saying, *"You also go and work in my vineyard, and I will pay you whatever is right"* (v.4).

At about the sixth hour and the ninth hour he did the same thing. Then, at *"the eleventh hour he went out and found still others standing around. He asked them, 'Why have you been standing here all day long doing nothing?' "Because no one has hired us," they answered. He said to them, 'You also go and work in my vineyard'"* (vv.6-7).

At day's end, when everyone was being paid, the men were surprised to learn they had all been paid the same wage – regardless of the hours they had toiled. The workers hired early in the morning began to grumble and complain, *"'These men who were hired last worked only one hour,' they said, 'and you have made them equal to us who have borne the burden of the work and the heat of the day'"* (Matthew 20:12).

The landowner answered one of them, *"Friend, I am not being unfair to you. Didn't you agree to work for a denarius? Take your pay and go. I want to give the man who was hired last the same as I gave you. Don't I have the right to do what I want with my own money? Or are you envious because I am generous?"* (Matthew 20:(vv.13-15).

Jesus told the story to make this point: *"So the last will be first, and the first will be last"* (Matthew 20:16).

A FULL REWARD

This is important: *Even if you do not come into an understanding of God's plan until the last hour, He will fulfill His promise for your life – and you will receive the full reward.*

Of course you want to know the mind of God sooner, so that you have more time to understand and act upon it. Regardless, the Lord will not allow you to be cheated out of what is rightfully yours.

No matter how many hurdles may be placed in your path, the same Lord who chose you will inspire you to rise above them. As one man told me, "You are on the road to success when you realize that failure is merely a detour."

God sees you as His triumphant heir – walking in the power of the Holy Spirit, completing the tasks He has assigned you.

The reason the Father sees victory is because His son has already conquered sin, death and the grave. Jesus overcame every obstacle, and we are complete in Him

The Bible tells us, *"But if the Spirit of him that raised up Jesus from the dead dwell in you, he that raised up Christ from the dead shall also quicken your mortal bodies by his Spirit that dwelleth in you"* (Romans 8:11).

As a partaker of the New Covenant, God has given you the strength to overcome. The revelation of John includes you when it says, *"He who has an ear, let him hear what the Spirit says to the churches. To him who overcomes, I will give some of the hidden manna. I will also give him a white stone with a new name written on it, known only to him who receives it."* (Revelation 2:17 NIV).

God's Spirit gives you the power to resurrect every vision the Lord has given – even those you received long ago and failed to act upon. It's not too late! *"Is anything too hard for the Lord?"* (Genesis 18:14).

His mark is upon you,
His Spirit is in you and your
inheritance is ahead of you!

CHAPTER 8

A MAN WITH A
VISION CANNOT DIE!

*I*t was just after Easter, 2000. We had experienced a phenomenal outpouring of God's Spirit on our church – record-breaking crowds and many coming to Christ.

Two days later, on Tuesday, I decided to get some exercise and teach my son, Sean, that I could still beat him in basketball. After all, I did play hoops in college, even though I was the shortest player on the team.

It was about 3:30 P.M. on a hot afternoon and I was trying to live up to my youthful reputation.

In the middle of the game, my father came out of the house, looked at me and said, "You need to take it easy. You're really sweating!"

"Don't worry. I'm okay," I responded, as dad climbed into his car and drove off.

A few minutes later, while we were still shooting baskets, I began to feel a slight upset in my stomach. "I'm going inside to get a little water and sit down for a bit," I told Sean. "But I'll be back to finish beating you!"

After a drink, I was still queasy and decided to go upstairs and take a shower. While showering, I began to feel a tightness in my chest – and my arms began to hurt.

Instinctively, I thought, "My grandfather died of a heart attack. So did my mother. And my dad has had *two* heart attacks." I told myself, "Hey dummy! You're having a heart attack!"

"WE HAVE TO DO SOMETHING!"

I was perspiring profusely, and things were getting worse, as I walked downstairs. I said to my daughter, Heather,

"Call mom. See if you can find her.
I think I'm having a heart attack!
We have to do something."

My wife was at the hair salon when her cell phone began ringing. Of course. I didn't want to call an ambulance – too embarrassing for the neighbors to see. How foolish!

People from the church staff arrived in an instant and rushed me to the hospital, while my wife and brother were converging on the scene.

"Get the cardiac team!" a hospital nurse ordered the minute I arrived. Immediately, four or five people began feverishly working on me in the emergency room. "Do you mind if we cut your clothes off?" a doctor politely asked?

"Cut them!" I responded. Who cares about clothes when you are dying?

"This may hurt," said a nurse, "but we've got to get an IV in you."

She was right! I felt the pain. They also gave me a shot to

open up the arteries to get the blood flowing. "Whatever you have to do," I told her.

At this point I was fully aware of what was going on – and could see my family and friends who had gathered nearby. Then, like a camera lens going out of focus, the people I was watching seemed to fade in and out. "Wow!" I thought, "Maybe they gave me something that's causing me to hallucinate."

The last thing I remember was a doctor saying, "We're losing him!"

"IT'S NOT COMPLETE!"

Suddenly, my physical senses were gone and it seemed that a video of my life began to play in front of me. I watched with amazement as it showed scenes of my life – from the time I was a little boy to the Easter services we had just enjoyed.

Still out of touch with the real world, I thought, "I feel good about this. God has been gracious to me and I have done what He called me to do." Then something jolted me and I said, "But God, when You gave me the vision for the church, what you showed me is not complete."

At that very moment, I heard the doctor say, "He's back! He's back!"

They had me upside down in the bed with my head facing the floor. When the attendants turned me around, the world tumbled back into focus.

Here is what I learned from that experience. As long as I remained true to the vision God called me to, the enemy couldn't kill me. Nothing in this world could alter the destiny God birthed in me. That is why I say: *A man with a vision cannot die!*

Why is this true? Because:

- You can't kill a man with a vision.
- You can't stop what God has started.
- You can't defeat what the Lord has raised up!

When we capture the mind of God and see what He has planned for us, there is nothing that can stop it! You cannot kill a man or woman who is walking in the presence and power of a Holy God.

HE WILL FULFILL IT

You may say, "Pastor, aren't you overlooking the fact that everyone – even *good people* – will die?"

Of course, I understand that. Here is what I am saying: *What God ordains for you, He will fulfill through you.*

Just having a vision is not enough. You also must have God's wisdom to know how to handle that revelation. When we talk about a person with a vision that cannot die; this is a man or woman who is walking in wisdom to *fulfill* the Father's plan.

The apostle Paul prayed, *"That the God of our Lord Jesus Christ, the Father of glory, may give unto you the spirit of wisdom and revelation in the knowledge of him"* (Ephesians 1:17).

That is powerful! God will give you these gifts so that you may have the knowledge of Jesus.

We talk about Him, but do we really *know* Jesus? We understand that He is the Son of the Living God who was born of a virgin, lived a sinless life and died on the cross for our sins. However, there is so much more to know of Christ. Paul tells us we need to have a revelation of these things.

DIVINE INSIGHT

The wisdom Paul spoke of is more than the ability to understand what is occurring; it tells us how to deal with circumstances. It is a skill.

I was watching a television program that showed riots occurring around the world. Policemen were well aware of what was taking place, but were unable to control the situation. It was unbelievable chaos! People were going absolutely crazy while the police stood helplessly by.

It is not enough to just have an understanding of what is happening. We need the wisdom to know how to deal with it!

> *Paul not only prayed for wisdom,
> but for revelation – divine insight.*

The apostle was not talking about physical insight, because he was speaking of Jesus. He prayed we would have the talent and skill, and know what to do with them.

Jesus once asked His disciples, *"Who do people say the Son of Man is?"* (Matthew 16:13 NIV).

They replied, *"Some say John the Baptist; others say Elijah; and still others, Jeremiah or one of the prophets"* (v.14).

He turned to Peter and asked, *"But what about you?"*... *"Who do you say I am?"* (v.15).

Simon Peter answered, *"You are the Christ, the Son of the living God"* (v.16).

What was the response of Jesus? He said, *"Blessed are you, Simon son of Jonah, for this was not revealed to you by man, but by my Father in heaven"* (v.17).

It was a revelation of the Spirit!

143

BEYOND GOALS

In today's society – including the church – we have taken the world's understanding of goals and called that vision. It's not true! Goals are nothing more than stepping stones. Vision deals with what God has placed you on this earth to do and complete that He might *celebrate* you.

Capturing God's dream for your life will cause Him to be glorified. That is why He will allow you to live to its completion.

What we are talking about is spiritual, not carnal. Vision is not something you devise. The psalmist wrote, *"Delight thyself also in the Lord; and he shall give thee the desires of thine heart"* (Psalms 37:4).

Desire is nothing more than goals – it is not revelatory insight or vision. Yet how are they attained? By delighting in the Lord.

We must be guided by the Spirit. As Paul wrote, *"For as many as are led by the Spirit of God, they are the sons of God"* (Romans 8:14). And we are told, *"For to be carnally minded is death; but to be spiritually minded is life and peace"* (Romans 8:6).

Our body is the Temple of the Holy Ghost. *"But we have this treasure in earthen vessels, that the excellency of the power may be of God, and not of us"* (2 Corinthians 4:7).

If we are going to be people of success in the Kingdom of God, we must step into the spirit realm. It is a place most people have never been.

THE RIGHT CHOICES

The Bible declares, *"Where there is no vision, the people perish: but he that keepeth the law, happy is he"* (Proverbs 29:18). If those same words were reversed, that scripture would read: *"With a vision, you will not die!"*

The Amplified Bible says it this way: *"Where there is no vision [no redemptive revelation of God], the people perish"* (v.18 AMP). In other words, where there is no spiritual insight of God's deliverance there is no life.

Being led by the Spirit (not the flesh) means that when I face a problem I realize that God has a way by which I can either overcome, conquer or escape from. I must decide which it is – and that comes from having the mind of God and being led by the Spirit.

Sometimes the Lord wants you to possess the mountain. Other times He wants you to toss it into the sea. Or, He may want you to be tolerant of certain things.

It is His divine wisdom and revelation that allows you to make the right choice.

David had a difficult time dealing with this. Saul kept trying to kill him, but God said to David, "Don't fight or harm Saul. Just tolerate him. I will make a way of escape for you."

To the very man who was trying to take his life, David kept playing his harp and singing his songs. That's what can result from spiritual insight.

IS IT OF GOD?

If I want to become an independently wealthy person, I set my hand to go into business. That is okay, yet it is natural, not spiritual. Thus it is *temporal!* The Bible says, *"But the natural man receiveth not the things of the Spirit of God: for they are foolishness unto him: neither can he know them, because they are spiritually discerned"* (1 Corinthians 2:14).

145

God's Spirit will reveal what He has prepared for us. Jesus clearly said, *"...when he, the Spirit of truth, is come, he will guide you into all truth: for he shall not speak of himself; but whatsoever he shall hear, that shall he speak: and he will show you things to come. He shall glorify me: for he shall receive of mine, and shall show it unto you"* (John 16:13-14).

Jesus also told us, *"If ye shall ask any thing in my name, I will do it"* (John 14:14). Then He added, *"If ye love me, keep my commandments"* (John 14:15).

The Word is there to confirm what the Spirit has shown you. Otherwise, it is not of God.

Jesus said the Spirit would reveal *all* things to you, yet He doesn't speak for Himself – but for the Father.

WHOSE SCHEDULE?

God has a calendar for your life. The Bible says, *"To every thing there is a season, and a time to every purpose under the heaven: A time to be born, and a time to die; a time to plant, and a time to pluck up that which is planted"* (Ecclesiastes 3:1-2).

A person who is fulfilling God's vision will be taken to heaven only on His schedule.

You have a *time!* Scripture tells us, *"...it is appointed unto men once to die"* (Hebrews 9:27). Yet, you do not have to die too soon – or too sick. It is God's decision.

You also don't have to die old! I'm not talking about the age on your birth certificate, rather the way you act or think.

I remember taking my father for his annual checkup. In the waiting room he looked a little upset. I asked, "What's wrong?"

"Look at all these old people in here," he responded.

I said, "Dad, you're 83 years old!"

"I'm not talking about numerical years," he said. "Look at them! They act old, they walk old, they talk old. I need to get out of here! They're getting on my nerves!"

FOLLOWING THE CALL

The reason people of vision cannot die before their time is because they must complete what God has called them to do. You may say, "I know some missionaries who died in a plane crash."

So do I. Yet, when I checked the facts I learned they were in an overloaded aircraft, or tried to fly in a storm. When that happens you can't say, "God took them." No. The devil didn't take them either. They made a human mistake.

In perilous circumstances, unless you have a sovereign word from God to go, you had better stay put.

I have been in situations where I could have been killed at any moment. It didn't bother me at all because I knew God had clearly said, "You are to go and do this."

I wasn't there because I wanted to be. It was because God told me – and He gave my life protection.

THEY CAPTURED HIS MIND

The Bible is filled with stories of men and women of God who understood they were people of vision. As a result, their obstacles became stepping stones – opportunities to see the Lord perform what He promised.

Abraham Captured the Mind of God

The son of Abraham was placed on a sacrificial altar, yet Isaac didn't complain because he knew he was a child of promise. Abraham realized that even if the child died, he would be raised from the dead. God had said to him, *"It is*

147

through Isaac that your offspring will be reckoned" (Hebrews 11:18).

The only thing that mattered was what the Almighty said.

Moses Captured the Mind of God

Floating down the river, Moses found himself in a small ark made out of bull rushes. He was being hidden from Pharaoh. That's when God stepped in and raised him up to set the nation of Israel free.

Moses' vision was not to die under the hand of Pharaoh, or lose his life in the dessert. God revealed His will step by step. When Moses saw the burning bush which would not be consumed, he began to realize God's sustaining power.

Joshua Captured the Mind of God

At Jericho, Joshua faced a major obstacle. Yet, before the battle ever took place God showed him the outcome. The Lord said to Joshua, *"See, I have delivered Jericho into your hands"* (Joshua 6:2 NIV).

He was told to have his men march around the walls of the city for six days. And on the seventh day they were to *"march around the city seven times, with the priests blowing the trumpets. When you hear them sound a long blast on the trumpets, have all the people give a loud shout; then the wall of the city will collapse and the people will go up, every man straight in"* (vv.4-5).

That is exactly what occurred. Joshua not only captured the mind of God, he conquered the city!

Jesus Captured the Mind of God

The Son of God came into this world fully understanding what He must do. On the cross, with heaven and hell in the balance, Jesus looked up and said, *"Father, into thy hands I commend my spirit"* (Luke 23:46).

Jesus knew the will of His Father – He understood that in three days the world would see the fulfillment of the greatest vision mankind had ever known.

Paul Captured the Mind of God

Shipwrecked on an island, the apostle Paul was sitting by a fire when a venomous serpent reached out and latched onto him. The people gasped, yet Paul "...shook the snake off into the fire and suffered no ill effects" (Acts 28:5 NIV).

Why was he so calm? He knew the mission to which God had assigned him. The apostle said, "I have not completed my course. I've not run my race. There is still something left for me to do!"

Peter Captured the Mind of God

In the middle of a storm, the disciples saw Jesus walking on the water. Peter said, *"Lord, if it be thou, bid me come unto thee on the water"* (Matthew 14:28).

When Peter stepped out of the boat he looked at the boisterous waves and began to sink. Yet, he had enough sense to look back at Jesus – the author and finisher of his faith.

It was by renewing his trust in the Lord that he was saved.

WHAT ABOUT YOU?

I believe it is time for you to see the miraculous power of the Almighty manifested in your life.

When God gives you His vision:

- Like Isaac, you will present yourself as a living sacrifice.
- Like Moses, you will experience God's sustaining power.

- Like Joshua, you will see the walls come crumbling down.
- Like Jesus, you will place your life in the Father's hands.
- Like Paul, you will shake off the enemy's attacks.
- Like Peter, you will step out of your boat and trust the Lord.

God is looking for a people He can raise up and place His Spirit within. When that happens, you will not be destroyed, because He has a plan for your life.

FIVE VITAL STEPS

The process of capturing the mind of God – and receiving His vision for your future – involves these five steps:

Step one: Declaration

Open your life to the declaration of God's Word. It unveils the Father's plan for your life. *"The spirit of man is the candle of the Lord, searching all the inward parts of the belly"* (Proverbs 20:27). The Word penetrates your entire being.

Step two: Impartation

Declaration creates impartation. The Lord will begin to speak to you – and give divine insight. When you receive God's Word, it will produce spiritual revelations. You will begin to understand what *"Eye hath not seen, nor ear heard"* (1 Corinthians 2:9).

Step three: Transformation

When the Word is declared to your spirit and is imparted into your life, you cannot remain the same. You are a changed person. *"And ye shall know the truth, and the truth shall make you free"* (John 8:32).

- I cannot walk in darkness when I know there is light.
- I cannot walk in poverty when I know there is prosperity.
- I cannot walk in death when I know there is healing and life in Jesus Christ.
- I cannot walk in failure when I know there is success in God.
- I cannot walk in defeat when I know that God has called me to be more than a conqueror.

When these things are declared to you and God imparts His purpose for your life, you will be changed – from glory to glory!

Step four: Manifestation

After taking the first three steps you are ready to see the tangible results. God's revelation gives you a title deed to your manifestation. After Jesus told the parable of seed (the Word) being sown on good ground, He declared *"For there is nothing hid, which shall not be manifested"* (Mark 4:22).

Step five: Celebration

I believe people lose their blessing because they don't celebrate what the Lord has done. Our God is a jealous God and will share His glory with no one. If we fail to praise Him, the Lord has the right to take back what He has given.

Years ago, when I was a youth pastor, a man in our congregation attended a Kathryn Kuhlman meeting and received his sight after being blind for ten years due to sugar diabetes. It was a miracle!

The next Sunday we didn't see him in church and wondered what happened to him. Three weeks later we received a call from his wife and she was weeping as she told us, "He has gone blind again."

We visited him and asked, "Why haven't we seen you in church? Where have you been?"

His wife took us aside and told us that when he received his healing he came home and watched television ten to twelve hours a day – and wouldn't leave the house.

What a lesson! If you want to walk in the miraculous, learn what God requires. Celebrate what the Lord has done.

KEEPING THE VISION ALIVE

A man recently asked me, "Pastor, I believe the Lord has shown me what the future holds, but how do I keep the vision alive and fresh?"

Based on God's Word, here is what I recommend:

1. Keep your focus.

When the Lord reveals your purpose in life, stay on course. Be like the person written about by the psalmist: *"He shall not be afraid of evil tidings: his heart is fixed, trusting in the Lord"* (Psalms 112:7)

Don't be tempted to chase ten or twenty dreams. Choose the one thing God reveals.

The Bible says, *"A double minded man is unstable in all his ways"* (James 1:8).

Not everybody is going to understand what God has shown you. Some of the very people you think are your best friends may become your greatest enemies. That is why you must keep your eye on the heavenly prize.

2. Stay pure.

You can't afford unforgiveness, anger or bitterness to seep into your life. Jesus said, *"Blessed are the pure in heart: for they shall see God"* (Matthew 5:8).

Sin destroys purity – and it must not stand between you and the Lord. You may ask, "What is sin?" It is anything that causes you to neglect your walk with God. Oh, we like to attack certain behaviors such as drugs and alcohol. In the process we have tried to make the fruit the *root*. No. The root of sin is rebellion against God. *"Therefore to him that knoweth to do good, and doeth it not, to him it is sin"* (James 4:17).

Practice purity.

3. Stay obedient.

God's vision for your life is sustained through obedience. Jesus declared, *"He that hath my commandments, and keepeth them, he it is that loveth me"* (John 14:21).

After the rebellion of the 1960s, parents shied away from the biblical principle to *"Train up a child in the way he should go: and when he is old, he will not depart from it"* (Proverbs 22:6).

This lack of discipline has resulted in a culture that says, "If I don't want to do it, I don't have to!"

I am convinced the reason we don't see more miracles in our churches is because they are filled with disobedient children. They refuse to tithe, fail to read the Word, and spend little time in prayer.

There is only one way to see God's will completed in your life: start walking in obedience.

4. Stay in love.

What do I mean? The Bible tells us that we overcome the

world by our faith, and that *"The only thing that counts is faith expressing itself through love"* (Galatians 5:6 NIV).

Love is the energizing factor.

Unfortunately, our society has taught people just the opposite – to be selfish, stingy and vindictive. It is time for the church to say, "I am going to love despite what anybody else says or does. I will be a man who gives, who encourages."

Love gives us the ability to properly fulfill God's promise to Adam in the book of Genesis – that we have dominion over the earth.

5. Keep walking in faith.

We have a tendency to talk about faith, but not live by it. Faith means I have to believe God for something I can't do. How is that possible? Constantly keep things in your life that are unobtainable on your own – it will keep you on the "faith line."

Someone told me, "Pastor, I'd love to be a partner in the ministry, but I just can't afford it."

That's the point! You must step out in faith and go beyond the natural. Start with the small things. Believe God to heal your headache – don't wait until you have a major problem. Remember, *"...without faith it is impossible to please him: for he that cometh to God must believe that he is, and that he is a rewarder of them that diligently seek him"* (Hebrews 11:6).

He rewards you with His vision.

6. Stay generous.

The only way to make room for an infilling, is to have an outflowing! That means we must be givers, not takers. *"Knowing that whatsoever good thing any man doeth, the same shall he receive of the Lord"* (Ephesians 6:8).

We serve a generous God. The Bible says, *"For God so*

WITH A VISION, YOU CANNOT DIE!

loved the world, that he gave... "(John 3:16).

Ephesians 5 tells us we are to imitate the Lord – to shower love on our husband or wife, just as Christ loved the church.

Generosity opens the floodgates of heaven, for *"God loves a cheerful giver"* (2 Corinthians 9:7).

THE COMPLETED PICTURE

As you capture the mind of God, every part of life's puzzle will finally fit together. When that last piece is in place, what a picture you will behold.

We know that, *"Eye hath not seen, nor ear heard, neither have entered into the heart of man, the things which God hath prepared for them that love him. But God hath revealed them unto us by his Spirit: for the Spirit searcheth all things, yea, the deep things of God"* (1 Corinthians 2:10).

MY PRAYER FOR YOU

As I write these words the Lord has directed me to prophesy over your life. This is the blessing I see God giving you:

> *By the power and authority given me through the name and the blood of Jesus Christ our Savior, I see you now standing in front of the Father and He is saying, "Well done good and faithful servant. You were faithful in the small things, I gave you larger, and you were obedient and committed to your God-given vision. You have accomplished all that I required of you and have given glory to My name. You will be rewarded and rule with me eternally." Yes, your Heavenly home*

155

awaits you and as it was said to Father Abra-
ham, "And so, after he had patiently endured,
he obtained, the promise" (Hebrews 6:15).

As a result of reading this book:
- I pray that you have come into agreement with the Father concerning His purpose for your life.
- I pray you will have a passion for His will to be totally accomplished.
- I pray you will be committed to God, your family and your church as you see the vision fulfilled.

Finally, *I pray you will never stop seeking to capture the mind of God.*

Resources

Avanzini, John, *Moving the Hand of God*. Harrison House, 1990.

Avanzini, John, *Rich God, Poor God*. International Faith Center, Inc., 2001.

Barnett, Matthew, *The Church that Never Sleeps*. Thomas Nelson Publishers, 2000.

Blackaby, Henry T. and King, Claude V., *Experiencing God*. Lifeway Press, Inc.1990.

Capps, Charles, *Releasing the Ability of God*. Harrison House, 1978.

Fortune, Don and Katie, *Discover Your Spiritual Gifts*.

Full Life Study Bible, NIV, Zonverdan, 1983.

Hebrew Greek Study Bible, NIV. AMG International, Inc. 1996.

Hibbert, Albert, *SmithWigglesworth, The Secret of His Power*. Harrision House, 1982.

Joyner, Rick, *The Harvest*. Morningstar Publication, Inc., 1989.

Kenyon, E.W., *Identification-A Romance of Rredemption*. Kenyon's Gospel Publications Society, 1998.

Maxwell, John C., *Your Road Map for Success*. Maxwell Motivation, Inc., 2002.

Mirnirth, Frank, and Littleton, Mark. *You Can*. Thomas Nelson Publications, 1994.

Murdock, Mike. *The Law of Recognition*. Wisdom International, 1999.

Ogilvie, Lloyd John, *Discovering God's Will in Your Life*. Harvest House Publisher, 1982.

Patterson, Ben, *Waiting*. Intervarsity Press, 1989.

Shaping History through Prayer and Fasting, (Appendix No, 7&8, Volume 12,13 – U. S. Statues at Large).

Prince, Derek, *Blessings or Curses, You Can Choose*. Chosen, 1990.

Roberts, Oral, *Miracle of Seed Faith*. Oral Roberts Evangelistic Association.

Sandford, John & Paula, *Healing the Wounded Spirit*. Victory House, Tulsa. Okla., 1985.

Sandford, John & Paula, *Restoring the Christian Family*

Smalley, Gary, *Joy That Lasts*. Zondervan, 1986.

Sheets, Dutch, *Intercessory Prayer*. Regal Books, 1996.

Towns, Elmer L., *Praying the Lord's Prayer*. Regal Books, 1973.

Willis, Paul C., *Whoosh-When the Spirit Comes*. Christian Word Publications, 1994.

BOOKS, TAPES AND VIDEOS BY
RICK THOMAS

THE VISION WORKBOOK
A companion to Capturing the Mind of God.
Includes a comprehensive outline and study helps.

TITHE, THE COVENANT CONNECTION
An audio series and workbook that will give you spiritual
insight and a breakthrough in finances.

SEVEN STEPS TO ABUNDANCE
Seven booklets and an audio series designed to
help you open the door to God's blessing.

A MAN WITH A VISION CANNOT DIE
In this exciting video, Dr. Thomas shares his
personal life and near-death experience to give
you hope and build your faith.

A SIGNIFICANT SEED AND A PERPETUAL HARVEST
An important video that explains how the seed
we sow can have a meaningful, lasting benefit.

To order these and other materials, contact:

DR. RICK THOMAS
ABUNDANT LIFE CHRISTIAN CENTRE
1490 BANKS ROAD
MARGATE, FL 33063